THE BUMPER BOOK OF QUESTIONS AND ANSWERS

D1495752

CLIVEDEN PRESS

INTRODUCTION

What is dry ice?

Do flowers grow in the desert?

How do you milk a snake?

How does a ball-point pen work?

Find the answers to all these questions and many more besides in this interesting and informative new annual. It covers topics like people and places, nature, science, art, geography, music and general knowledge. Open the book at any page and learn something new about the world about you, or the world as it was. Broaden your mind and astonish your friends with the facts at your fingertips.

As you look through the book you will see that symbols are introduced on some of the question and answer pages. These symbols tell you into which category the questions fall, and whether they are of interest to boys, girls, or both. This is what they mean:

Boy – questions of interest to a boy
Girl – questions of interest to a girl
Flower – Nature
Microscope – Science
Sun – Weather
Globe – Geography
Castle – History

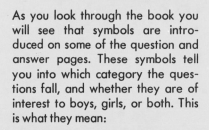

WHAT ARE THE GREAT LONDON LIVERY COMPANIES?

In medieval times, craftsmen banded together to form craft guilds, to decide on terms of apprenticeship and employment, and to guarantee conditions and high standards of workmanship. Survivors of these craft guilds, there are now twelve Great London Livery Companies, each having its own Royal charter and the right to bear arms.

The Skinners traded in animal skins, and sold fur garments. In the Middle Ages only the nobility were allowed to wear furs, so furs were an important and valuable commodity.

MERCERS

SKINNERS

The Mercers traded in a wide variety of goods, from fabrics to small pieces of jewellery. They were the first of the twelve Great Guilds, first mentioned in the early 1100s.

The Goldsmiths still hallmark gold, even today, to guarantee its quality. Every year, at Goldsmiths' Hall, new coins from the Royal Mint are delivered in a sealed box called the Pyx, and they are then weighed and tested for accuracy. This has happened ever since the 13th century.

GOLDSMITHS

EVERYDAY THINGS

Who was the first person to carry an umbrella regularly in England as a protection against the rain?

Although sunshades were used from early times in the east it was a man named Jonas Hanway who started to carry an umbrella about with him through the streets of London on rainy days around the mid 18th century. Poor Jonas was greatly mocked for this. Small boys followed him about jeering at him ... but while *they* got wet, *he* kept dry. Today a man carries an umbrella with him as naturally as he does his briefcase.

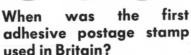

When was the first adhesive postage stamp used in Britain?

It was a Penny Black bearing a portrait of Queen Victoria. It was issued in May 1840 when Rowland Hill initiated several postal reforms. It was not perforated, but had to be cut from a printed sheet. Today the Penny Black stamp is very valuable indeed. The introduction of the stamp also called for the invention of postboxes, which were introduced in 1855.

What is a sponge?

A sponge is usually a marine animal found clinging to the underside of a rock. There are three kinds of sponges: limy, with needles making up the sponge's body; glass sponges found in the tropics with beautiful glassy spikes, and horny sponges which are of the most commercial value. The Common Household Sponge is the skeleton of a certain kind of sponge with all the living animal tissue removed.

How does a ball-point pen work?

The tip of a ball-point pen is a rotating metal ball which is made of a material which grips the paper when writing. It is held in place by a *seat* which is a kind of socket, so that the ball rotates as you write. As it rotates the ball picks up ink from an ink cartridge and so writing appears on the paper.

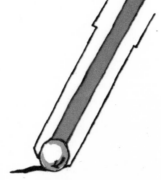

What was the penny farthing an early form of?

The bicycle. Penny farthings appeared in 1870 and three years later a safety penny farthing with a chain to the rear wheel was developed. Later, in 1888, a Scottish vet named

John Boyd Dunlop fitted the first pneumatic tyres to a bicycle; then came the free wheels, and just before the turn of the century variable gears were introduced.

How long have people been using buttons?

Since as early as the 13th century when they were often used as bone ornaments rather than for buttoning a garment as they are used today. Although usually round, buttons can be almost any shape, size or colour. Sets of buttons were given as gifts during the 18th and 19th century and a New York firm have made buttons from tagua nuts which harden when they are heated. Pearl buttons come from certain oyster and mussel shells. In China a literary honour is bestowed on someone by the placing of a gold button in his cap, while Mandarins wear a different button on the top of their caps.

Who invented the first thermos flask?

Sir James Dewar, in the year 1892. It consists of a double-walled flask with a vacuum between the walls. The walls are silvered and heat cannot be conducted across a vacuum. They keep hot liquids hot because the heat cannot get out and cold liquids cold because heat cannot get in. After the liquid has been poured in, a cork stopper is used to seal the flask as cork is a very poor conductor of heat.

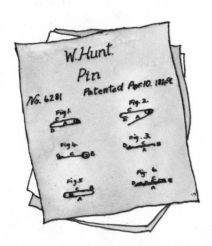

What well-known everyday object did Walter Hunt invent?

By bending a piece of wire into an unusual but safe shape, Walter Hunt rediscovered a simple device used thousands of years ago: the safety pin. Three years later, in 1849, Hunt obtained the patent for his new discovery, having supplied the Patents Office with a sketch and description of his wonderful new invention, which in fact had been used by the ancient Romans to hold up their togas!

QUESTIONS AND ANSWERS

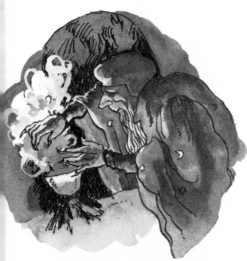

Why were American soldiers in World War II called G.I.s?

World War Two was the time that this nickname originated, although it has since stuck and most soldiers are called by this name now. During that war all government kits supplied to recruits in the American Army were stamped 'G.I.' meaning 'Government Issue'. It was as rather a cynical joke that the soldiers began calling themselves G.I.s, meaning that they thought themselves little more important than their equipment. Before this, from about 1850 until the First World War, the American soldiers had called themselves 'Dough boys', because they wore uniforms with metal buttons which looked like round cakes of dough.

What was Alchemy?

Alchemy was an ancient science, practised from A.D. 500 up until the Middle Ages, when men believed they could turn base metals into gold, if only they were able to find the right formula and the 'philosopher's stone'. Alchemists were the forerunners of the chemists we know today, but they also dabbled in astrology and spiritualism to try to achieve their aims of making gold and finding the secrets of eternal youth. The earliest alchemists were the Ancient Egyptians.

How is fog formed?

Water vapour is always around us in the atmosphere, in varying amounts according to pressure and temperature. When the temperature drops suddenly, these water vapour particles condense on the dust specks in the air, and this produces the haze we call 'fog'.

'Smog' is a combination of smoke and fog, and is a particular menace in the industrial cities of America, but surprisingly it's Athens in Greece which suffers badly from smog. Smog eats away at the classical Greek buildings there, such as the Parthenon, at an amazing rate, causing serious damage.

Who were the Suffragettes?

They were a group of women at the beginning of this century who fought for women's rights, especially the right of women to vote. Mrs. Emmeline Pankhurst, along with her daughter Christabel and friend Annie Kenney, had to fight Parliament, public opinion and even go to prison before women were given equal rights with men to vote on the affairs of the country. The Representation of the People Act in 1918 meant that some women got the vote, mainly because public opinion was better disposed towards women after their help with the war effort, but it wasn't until 1928 that every woman over 21 was able to vote. The women who had fought for this were called 'Suffragettes' because they belonged to the Women's Suffrage Movement. 'Suffrage' means the right to vote.

What is the origin of the Marathon race?

The Marathon is a long, gruelling race which traditionally closes the Olympic events. It is taken from the amazing achievement of the Greek runner Pheidippides, who ran over twenty-six miles in four hours, taking news to Athens of the Persians' defeat at the Battle of Marathon in 490 B.C.

Do budgerigars really talk?

Budgies, like the other members of the parrot family, have surprising powers of mimicry and extremely retentive memories, so 'talking' comes fairly easily to them – but of course they have no idea what it is that they are actually repeating! They simply pick up sounds and imitate them, often catching the tone of voice and pronunciation perfectly. It's quite easy to train your budgie to say simple sentences, but don't expect him to hold a conversation with you! Budgerigars were originally green in their natural state, but breeding has meant that they are all the colours of the rainbow these days.

Who invented the thermometer?

Galileo, the Italian scientist, invented the thermometer in 1593. At that time, however, it was used to measure pressure changes in relation to weather predictions, rather than to take a human temperature!

What was the Blitz?

The Blitz was a massive air assault on London by German bombers and it began in September 1940, when nine hundred German aircraft bombed London's dockland, setting most of the East End ablaze. Many further attacks followed, destroying historical monuments and homes, causing great damage and loss of life. The firemen and voluntary helpers of London worked so hard and courageously that Winston Churchill called them 'the heroes with grimy faces'.

What was a Sedan chair?

A Sedan was a covered chair on two poles, which was carried through the streets by two men. The chair was box-shaped, with two windows and a door, and the roof was made so that it could be lifted should the passenger wish to stand in the chair – rather a dangerous thing to do! The porters carried the chair by the two long poles between which the chair was fixed, and this kind of transport was popular in the seventeenth and eighteenth centuries. The name comes from the French town of Sedan, where this kind of transport is said to have originated.

9

What was the tyrannosaurus?

The tyrannosaurus was an immense dinosaur, measuring over forty-six feet tall! 'Dinosaur' means 'terrible lizard' and the tyrannosaurus was the most terrible dinosaur of all. One of the most fearsome and ferocious animals ever to roam the earth, these giant reptiles existed over 60,000,000 years ago during the Cretaceous period.

What are Kew Gardens?

The Royal Botanic Gardens are at Kew, in Surrey. Originally they were a nine acre botanical estate owned by Princess Augusta, widow of Frederick, Prince of Wales. Princess Augusta's son, George III, lived at Richmond Lodge nearby and later its land was to form the basis for Kew Gardens as we know it today. The Gardens were given over to the public in 1841, and in 1897 Queen Victoria gave the semi-uncultivated pastures of the Queen's Cottage to the Gardens. Today there are about three hundred acres of vast conservatories and botanical museums at Kew.

Who was Sir Isaac Newton?

Sir Isaac Newton is often considered to be the world's finest scientist. Born in Lincoln in 1642, he studied at Cambridge and went on to discover the law of gravitation, and invent the first reflecting telescope. He was knighted in 1702 and died in 1727. He is buried in Westminster Abbey. He wrote his masterpiece, *Principia*, in 1687.

What – and where – is the island of Surtsey?

A volcanic eruption occurred just off the southern coast of Iceland in 1963, throwing up a massive amount of ash, cinders and molten lava. The ash and cinders were carried by the waves and then floated to the seabed, but the lava settled on this bed of ashes, and began to harden and cool. This mass of once-molten lava has become hard as rock and is now an island – the island of Surtsey, with an area of about one square mile. Of course, it's not inhabited, but plant, insect and animal life is appearing there, making the island a fascinating place for scientists.

10

THE GAMES PEOPLE PLAY . . .

What is pelota?

Played mainly in France and Spain, and in North and Latin America, pelota is claimed to be the fastest of all ball games. It originated many thousands of years ago in South America, where it was played as a sacred game in the temples. It is played by two players against a wall, the small, hard rubber ball being hurled from, and caught in, a curved basket attached to each player's wrist. The ball is served from the basket, and his opponent must catch the ball on the volley or first bounce, and return it. A point is won when the receiver fails to catch and return the ball. In America pelota is also known as jai-alai.

What is knur and spell?

A word game? A Viking singing duo? A witch's curse? No, knur and spell is a little-known game that has been played in the Pennine area of Northern England for the last 300 years. The game has a terminology all its own. The knur is a small baked clay ball, sometimes known as a potty. The spell is a wooden structure something like a miniature gallows, from which the knur is suspended. The players—known locally as laikers —must hit the knur with a long sycamore cane, the laiker whose knur travels furthest being the winner. The game had almost died out until recently, but now there has been lots of new interest, and a world championship is planned.

What is pall-mall?

This game is similar to croquet, played with a wooden mallet and ball. The name derives from the Italian *palla* (ball) and *maglio* (mallet). Though not played much nowadays, pall-mall enjoyed great popularity in England, Italy and other parts of Europe in the 1600s.

V-V-VERY INTERESTING

What is Valhalla?

The word means *Hall of the Slain* and, in Norse mythology, was the great hall of the dead heroes. The hall had 540 doors, so wide that 800 men could enter side by side, and the guests were seated at long tables where they were served with wondrous foods and drink. Valhalla's walls were of gold, lined with battle shields so highly polished that the light they cast made candles unnecessary, and coats of mail and armour hung from the walls.

What is a vicuna?

The vicuna is a member of the camel family, found in the Andes Mountains of South America, usually above the snow line at heights of about 15,000 feet. Unlike the camel it has no hump, and grows to about three feet at the shoulder. It lives in small herds, eats grass and, thanks to its remarkable speed, endurance and keen eyesight, is rarley seen at close quarters. The vicuna has very fine fleece, which is made into top quality (and very expensive) cloth.

What is a verst?

A verst is a Russian measure of length, about ⅔ mile, though seldom used nowadays.

What is Vedic?

Vedic literature is the sacred literature of the Hindus. Its four main works are the *Rig Veda*, the *Sama Veda*, the *Yajur Veda* and the *Atharva Veda*. Each Veda contains collections of hymns called *Samhitas*, most of which were composed by unknown holy men as long as 4,000 years ago.

Ancient Vedic wisdom is recorded on palm-leaf books like this one.

Who are the Valkyries?

They were the warlike battle-maidens of Norse mythology who took the dead battle heroes to Valhalla, and waited upon them there. The name means *those who choose the fallen*. Richard Wagner based his famous opera *Die Walküre* on the story of one of the Valkyries, Brunhild, who was awakened from a magic sleep.

What is vanadium?

Discovered by Swedish chemist Nils Sefstrom in 1830, vanadium is a rare, silvery-white metallic element, and one of the hardest metals. Vanadium is added to steel for greater strength and elasticity, often used in car chassis, and is used widely in medicines. It is found in small amounts in the ores of copper, lead and iron, and Peru is a major producer.

What is volvox?

Volvox is probably the simplest living organism composed of a number of cells that show a common purpose. Volvox (Latin for *rolling*) is a plant, looking like a tiny green ball as big as this 'o'. If you look carefully into the surface of a freshwater pool or pond you will probably see, rolling through the water, tiny green balls—these are volvox.

What is Vega?

Vega is a star, the fifth brightest, and is often called the *arc light of the sky*. Vega will become the earth's pole star in something like 12,000 years time.

KINGS AND QUEENS

Question:

In 1013, a Danish king called Sweyn Forkbeard made himself king of England. Later his son became king, and he is remembered for something he *failed* to do. What was this and what was the king's name?

Answer:

His name was Canute and he failed to hold back the waves of the sea, thus proving to his foolish courtiers that even a king cannot hold back the forces of nature.

Question:

A king of Scotland was known as 'The Large Head' and married a pious queen named Margaret who was known for her saintly ways. Can you name the Scottish King?

Answer:

Malcolm Canmore.

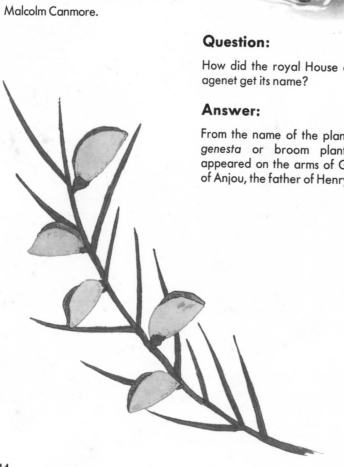

Question:

How did the royal House of Plantagenet get its name?

Answer:

From the name of the plant *planta genesta* or broom plant which appeared on the arms of Geoffrey of Anjou, the father of Henry II.

Question:

At what age did Queen Elizabeth I come to the throne of England?

Answer:

At the age of 25 years.

Question:

Can you give the full name of the British queen who was known as 'The Great White Queen' and say how many years she reigned?

Answer:

Alexandrina Victoria, daughter of Edward, Duke of Kent and Princess Victoria of Saxe-Coburg, who reigned for sixty-four years. Her reign started when she was 18 years of age and three years later, in 1840, she married her cousin, Prince Albert of Saxe-Coburg-Gotha.

Question:

Who was known as 'The King over the Water'?

Answer:

James II, after he was forced to flee to France, also the Old Pretender, his son James III, and his grandson, Charles Edward Stuart. When their Jacobite followers were asked to drink the loyal toast to the king, they passed their glasses first over a bowl of water before drinking, thus drinking not to George, but 'The King Over the Water'.

Question:

What are Eleanor Crosses?

Answer:

When his wife Eleanor of Castile died in 1290 at Hadbury in Nottinghamshire, Edward I wished her to be buried in Westminster Abbey and so the Queen's last journey was made, and at every place where her body rested, Edward had a cross put up to commemorate the spot. Three of these crosses still survive today, but originally there were twelve: at Lincoln, Grantham, Stamford, Geddington, Northampton, Stony Stratford, Woburn, Dunstable, St. Albans, Waltham, Cheapside and Charing Cross.

Question:

What is a 'Queen's Messenger'?

Answer:

The name given to an official of the British foreign office who carries secret diplomatic papers from London to embassies abroad. His emblem is a silver greyhound, and there have been Queen's Messengers dating back for several centuries.

IT'S A STRANGE WORLD!

When the railway was invented, people could not accustom themselves to the idea that there were no horses to pull the wagons and they still designed the coaches in the same way as the horse-drawn carriages. They looked exactly the same and there was even a holder in which to put the whip!

King James II debased England's coinage by issuing such worthless coins as brass pennines, half-pennies and farthings. A phrase indicating worthlessness was soon in use – 'Not worth a brass farthing'.

The bicycle as we know it today was invented in 1885 and was fitted with air-filled, pneumatic tyres by John Boyd Dunlop in 1888. They have covered many miles since then and the highest speed for cycling in one hour was recorded by a Frenchman in 1928 when he cycled 76 miles in the one hour, downhill presumably!

The Bedouin people really like to celebrate when they have a wedding feast. They eat the largest dish in the world, which is roasted camel prepared for the table by cooking eggs and stuffing them into fish, stuffing the cooked fish into roast chickens, stuffing the chickens into a cooked sheep, and stuffing the camel with the sheep!

Queen Elizabeth sent her seamen searching for the North-West Passage, exploring the Arctic, and sailing to distant lands, yet she herself never left England. The longest journey she made was to Bristol – 112 miles. She never even went to Wales or Scotland.

In days of old, pedlars used to collect the bread from a baker to sell at the market. In payment a pedlar would get an extra loaf from the baker for every twelve loaves he sold, making thirteen loaves in all. The number thirteen today is called the baker's dozen.

16

STARS AND STRIPES

What is a starfish?

A starfish is not a fish at all, it is a curiously beautiful sea animal with a body usually shaped like a five-pointed star, hence its name. But a starfish can have as many as forty arms, or rays as they are sometimes called. If one of these arms is chopped off, either by accident or design, then from this arm another starfish grows! Rather a strange way to regenerate, isn't it?

The starfish has peculiar tube-like feet which it often uses to open oysters, much to the annoyance of oyster fishers, especially as when the fishers think that they have caught a starfish, the latter just breaks off one of its arms and hurries away to catch more oysters!

What is the 'Star-Spangled Banner'?

The national anthem of the United States of America, which was written during the Anglo-American War of 1812 when, despite British bombardment, the American flag with its stars and stripes could still be seen flying at Fort McHenry as the Americans tried to protect Baltimore. The words were written by Francis Scott Key, who was a prisoner aboard a British ship. It was officially approved as the national anthem of the USA in 1931. Today the stars on the star-spangled banner number fifty, one for each state of the union, while the stripes represent the original number of the united states.

Where will you see Orion the hunter?

In the sky, as Orion is a constellation of stars above the celestial equator. In Greek mythology Orion was a mighty hunter, and when he was slain by Diana he was taken up to the heavens together with his dogs. The constellation contains the shoulder stars, Betelgeuse, an orange-red, first magnitude, irregular variable star, and Bellatrix, and the giant pure white star known as Rigel.

In which country would you see the zebra mouse?

This tiny creature with its black and brown stripes running down its back is now only found in Africa. As well as being known as the zebra mouse it is also called the striped fieldmouse. It is found in many regions, making its home in a grassy hollow, where it rests during the hot time of day, after a busy morning scampering about on the savannah. It goes searching for food in the form of pulses and grasses, but it is always wary of snakes or birds of prey for whom this little mouse makes an excellent meal!

Who is Shere-Khan?

Shere-Khan is the tiger, one of the many animals which appear in Rudyard Kipling's *Jungle Book* which tells of the adventures of Mowgli, a child brought up by Mother Wolf in the jungle. Mowgli grows up obeying the laws of the jungle and amongst his animal friends and enemies are Shere-Khan the tiger, Baloo the bear, Banderlog the monkey people and Rikki-Tikki-Tavi the mongoose.

ABC OF GEOGRAPHY

Artesian well

A well sunk in a deep water-trapping basin which produces a continued flow of water at the surface because the well forces the water upwards by being below the level of the water's source.

Beaufort Wind Scale

Admiral Sir Francis Beaufort devised an internationally accepted series of numbers to chart wind strengths in 1805. On the Beaufort scale, a light breeze at four to seven miles an hour is numbered 2; while a hurricane, going at over seventy-five miles an hour, is numbered 12.

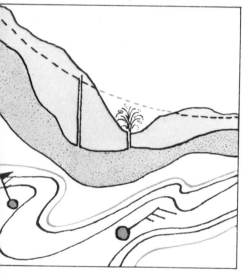

Capricorn, Tropic of

A line of latitude, 23 degrees 32' south of the Equator, where the sun shines directly overhead on December 21. The Tropic of Capricorn marks the southern boundary of the Tropical Zone.

Doldrums

Areas of the seas around the Equator with very low pressure and little wind. Sailing ships avoided the Doldrums for fear of being becalmed.

Estuary

The mouth of a river, usually broad and V shaped, formed by the sinking of coastal land as the river reaches the sea. When the tide comes in, sea and river mix.

Fiord

Long, narrow inlet of the sea, enclosed by cliffs, a fiord is supposed to be the result of glaciers moving seawards many years ago. The fiords of southern Norway are very beautiful.

Geyser

A hot spring which throws up steam and hot water into the air at regular intervals, geysers are common in Iceland and New Zealand.

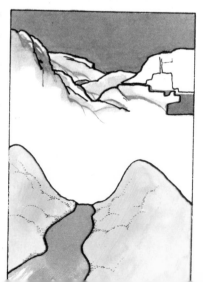

Hydrography

The science which deals with the surface waters of the earth, investigating tides and currents, the charting of coastlines and contributing to navigation.

Igneous rock

Rock that has solidified from molten rock (called magma). It is one of three kinds of rock that make up the earth's crust.

Jet stream

A westerly current of air moving between 60 and 270 miles an hour in the upper atmosphere.

Karst

A rugged landscape of dry valleys, caverns and underground streams made of limestone, occuring in Yugoslavia, the northern Pennines in England, and the Yucatan region of Mexico.

Levee

A high ridge or bank along the side of a river, made of material deposited on the side of the river after flooding. Artificial levees, of earth and sandbags, are made to contain a river during flooding.

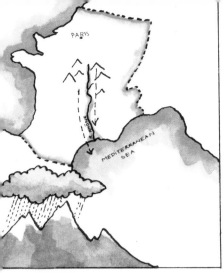

Mistral

A very cold wind which blows down over the Rhône valley from a high pressure area of central France to a low pressure area over the Mediterranean.

Neap tide

A tide with the smallest range between low and high water, occurring when the pull of the sun is at right angles to that of the moon.

Orographic rainfall

Rainfall over a mountain range, caused by moisture-laden air cooling and releasing its vapour as rain.

Pampas

The massive grasslands that surround the estuary of the Rio de la Plata in South America.

Quicksand

A mass of very deep, fine-grained sand that looks like ordinary sand but, when wet, will not support any weight at all and is a fatal menace for man and animals.

Rainbow

An arch of seven colours seen when sun follows rain. The raindrops reflect and refract the sun's rays, each becoming a prism. The colours are: red, orange, yellow, green, blue, indigo and violet.

Solstice

The time of year when the lengths of the days and nights are of the greatest difference. The summer solstice in the Northern Hemisphere is about June 21, the winter solstice around December 22. These dates are reversed in the Southern Hemisphere.

Tsunami

A Japanese word for great sea waves caused by submarine earthquakes, sweeping in from the ocean at up to 600 miles an hour and up to a hundred feet high, causing immense damage to coastal communities. These waves are often mistakenly called tidal waves.

Upland

Land that is higher than the surrounding region. Also called highland, as in the Highlands of Scotland.

Volcano

An opening in the earth's crust through which magma (molten rock, or lava) pours out. As this piles up and hardens around the opening, the familiar conical shaped hill is formed. An active volcano is one which erupts often, an extinct volcano is one that has not erupted since recorded history, and a dormant volcano is one which although not extinct, has not erupted for a long period.

Watershed

High land that separates river systems, the crest of the surrounding uplands that form the boundary of a river basin.

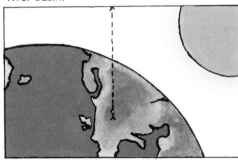

Year

The time taken by the earth to travel around the sun, measured by a calendar year of 365 days, adjusted from time to time for accuracy to 366 days.

Zenith

The point in the sky that is directly overhead from the observer's point of view. Nadir is its opposite, the point in space directly downwards from the zenith.

FACT OR FICTION?

DID ROBIN HOOD REALLY EXIST?

Opinions differ on the question of Robin Hood's existence. The earliest ballad about his life was written in the fifteenth century, almost 200 years after he was supposed to have lived, and some experts claim that Robin himself was no more than a ballad character invented to express the poor peasants' resentment over their unjust treatment.

However, there is earlier written evidence to suggest that there was such a man, although he was probably not the romantic character shown in the ballad. One document states that there was a *Robertus Hod, fugitivus,* (Robin Hood, outlaw) living in Yorkshire in the early thirteenth century, and it is worth remembering that Sherwood Forest extended into Yorkshire at that time.

WHO WAS ROB ROY?

According to Sir Walter Scott's novel, Rob Roy MacGregor was a dashing, courageous outlaw who robbed the rich to give to the poor. But, in fact, the real Rob Roy was more of an earlier Al Capone. He lived in Perthshire at the turn of the seventeenth century, and he ran a flourishing protection racket, charging other farmers large sums of money to protect their herds from cattle thieves. As Rob Roy was also one of the worst cattle thieves in Scotland they would not have had much faith in him, but to save themselves trouble they usually paid.

One of Rob Roy's greatest enemies was the Duke of Montrose, who had taken his property in payment for a debt. To take his revenge, Rob Roy and his followers raided the Duke's estates regularly, and terrorised the neighbourhood. Although captured by Montrose's men, Rob Roy managed to escape, and his daring and cunning soon made him a legendary figure.

WAS THERE REALLY A KING ARTHUR?

Although most of the legends surrounding King Arthur are untrue, Arthur himself did exist. It is doubtful that he was a king, but he was certainly a powerful leader of men, and he led them to victory against the invading Saxons who attacked Britain from all sides. At this time – the sixth century – Britain was divided into small kingdoms, but Arthur's victories brought stability and peace, and soon his name was known all over the country.

In the earliest records of Arthur, there is no mention of Guinevere, Sir Lancelot or the Knights of the Round Table. These were added much later when the legends took over from the facts. The court of Camelot is thought to have been at Cadbury Castle, in Somerset, where excavations have revealed a large earthwork hill-fort belonging to a powerful leader of the sixth century. As no other such stronghold has been found, this seems to be the most likely home of Arthur.

NURSERY RHYME PEOPLE AND PLACES

Many of our familiar nursery rhymes recall famous events or people in history. Do you know which nursery rhyme:

1. Recalls a famous churchman who was the son of an Ipswich butcher?

2. Recalls the days when the Pilgrims of the Mayflower copied a custom of the Indians concerning the care of young children?

3. Tells of Mistress Mary, so contrary, with her 'pretty maids'?

4. Recalls the days of the terrible plague, the symptoms of which were rosy rash?

5. Tells of a certain man of Glastonbury who took a special pie to King Henry VII at the time of the dissolution of the monasteries?

6. Recalls the struggle for power between Scotland and England, and the final unity of these two great countries?

7. Recalls a handsome young man with yellow hair whom the rhyme says is a sailor, but who was, in fact, a Parliamentary candidate during an 18th century election?

Check your answers on page 191

TELL ME, TELL ME

HOW DOES A SUBMARINE STAY UNDER WATER?

You may have noticed that an empty bottle will float along the surface of water, but one which is full of liquid will sink. The submarine works in exactly the same way. Each submarine has several large tanks, which can be filled with either water or air. When they are filled with air, the submarine will float on the surface of the water, just like a ship. When it is time for the submarine to dive, large amounts of water are pumped into the tanks, so making the vessel much heavier. By regulating the amount of water and air in the tanks, the crew of the submarine can make their vessel rise or sink to various levels in the water.

DO PLANTS EAT SOIL?

They certainly don't eat soil in the way that we eat various kinds of food, but it is in the soil that their roots search for the water and minerals which are vital for their health and growth. These minerals are transported to the various parts of the plants by the sap. The sap is a special liquid circulating all over the various parts of each plant. The plant also takes carbon dioxide from the air, and with the help of the energy of sunlight will convert it into sugars and other substances vital to healthy growth.

WHY DON'T MEN HAVE TAILS?

All species of animals, including man, of course, have developed very gradually over millions and millions of years. In this way, each animal strengthens and improves those parts of its body which are particularly useful, and the various parts which are not so useful diminish or are adapted. This evolution happens very, very slowly, and changes can only be seen over numerous generations. In four-legged animals, or quadrupeds as they are called, the tail is very important for balance, and in many cases it is used almost as another limb, for instance when monkeys swing through the trees. Man, however, walks on two legs – he is called a biped – and he does not need the tail for balance. As a matter of fact, a small very rudimentary 'tail' can be found at the base of our spines, but it does not help us at all with balance or movement.

WHY DOESN'T ONE KEY OPEN EVERY DOOR?

There wouldn't be much point in locking your door if you knew that anyone could come along with another key and *unlock* it! Locks and keys are made for keeping things safe from burglary or damage, and you should always lock up a house if you are going out, or a car if you are leaving it parked in a public place. There are many different shapes and sizes of keys, and each one fits into its own particular lock. The lock will be shaped inside

so that it will only take its own key. If a key is forced into it which does not fit exactly, the lock will not turn, and the door will stay shut. Unfortunately, many burglars learn various tricks by which they can force a lock open, and so anything which is particularly valuable is usually protected by other devices, such as alarms, 'combination' locks, or one of the most effective deterrents – a guard dog.

WHY DOESN'T THE SUN SHINE AT NIGHT?

Well, as a matter of fact the sun *is* shining at night, but we can't see it. The Earth, which is rotating in space, turns completely round once every twenty-four hours. In the course of this rotation each part of the globe will be facing the sun for a certain amount of time. It is this time which we call 'day'. When the part of the globe where we live is facing away from the sun, and we cannot see its light, we call the time 'night'. So, when it is day for you, it is night for many other people, far away in other lands.

HOW CAN WE HEAR THE SEA IN A SHELL?

Sad to say, it isn't really the sea which you can hear when you hold a shell up to your ear, even though it may sound exactly like it. What is really happening is this. . . . All sounds move through the air on vibrations of air called sound waves. We can't see sound waves moving, but even the tiniest sounds being made in a room will have their own sound waves. There is air too, of course, in the spiral cavity inside the shell, and when sound waves enter they make this air vibrate as they bounce backwards and forwards off the inner walls of the shell. The result is a deep rumbling sound from the air which is resounding inside the shell. This sound reminds us of the sound of waves beating on a shore. It is in just the same way as this that air vibrates inside the 'resonator' of musical instruments, making the sounds of the notes being played.

MORE QUESTIONS AND ANSWERS

WHAT IS QUICKSAND?

Quicksand is a loose, light sand mixed with water. It looks no different from ordinary sand, but it won't support any weight. Quicksand is usually found near the mouths of large rivers or flat shores where there is a stiff layer of clay below ground level. This clay stops the natural drainage of water, so the water collects in the sand. It's a common belief that quicksand will suck you under but, in fact, as the sand contains so much water, it's possible to float, as long as you move slowly. Moving slowly enables the sand to flow around the body and act like water in which you can swim.

WHAT WAS THE PONY EXPRESS?

In America, before the days of the railway and the telegraphs, the Government began a new system for carrying mail across the United States – from St. Joseph, Missouri, to the Pacific Ocean – which was known as the Pony Express. A number of horses carried the rider, with his mail bag, in a number of stages along the route. Each horse would travel ten or fifteen miles, and then a fresh horse would be saddled up and ridden away. The rider himself would travel three stages, or thirty miles, before being replaced with another rider. The riders had to brave Indian attacks, as well as all kinds of weather, to see the mail delivered, so they must have had great courage. They actually rode horses, not ponies, although they were called the Pony Express!

HOW DID CHESS BEGIN?

Chess is said to be the oldest game in the world, originating in India 5,000 years ago with the Buddhists, who, believing war to be wrong, devised the game of chess as a peaceful substitute. From India the game spread to Persia, Arabia and then to Western Europe. The word 'chess' is derived from the Persian word 'shah', meaning king, and 'check-mate', from 'shah mat', the king is dead. At one time the king could be captured, which would be impossible in today's game, and in ancient times the queen was the weakest piece on the board, only finding her present power 500 years ago. The method of 'castling' was introduced to the game 400 years ago, and the rook got its name from the Indian word 'ruhk', meaning soldier.

WHAT IS POMPEII?

Pompeii is an ancient Roman town in Italy, and an amazing thing happened there on August 24th, A.D. 79. The volcano Vesuvius erupted and lava completely buried the town. The lava, together with ashes and pebbles, fell dry on Pompeii and later, when water came down on top of this, the material became like plaster and formed moulds which preserved all that was underneath! In the Middle Ages this town was forgotten, until in 1594 an underground aqueduct was discovered and interest re-kindled in the town. Excavating has been going on ever since and Pompeii has become valuable – and infinitely fascinating – evidence of the past.

WHAT ANIMAL CAN RUN FASTEST?

Would you believe that man, and an elephant, can actually run up to twenty-five miles an hour, if running for a very short distance? The race horse, traditionally a fast animal, can reach fifty miles an hour, and a greyhound up to thirty-five miles an hour. The fastest animals, however, are wild in the bush; the antelope and gazelle can run up to sixty-five miles an hour, for a run of a mile or so. The fastest animal is, of course, the cheetah or hunting leopard, which can run at a maximum speed of seventy miles an hour!

WHAT WAS THE KINGDOM OF ATLANTIS?

Atlantis is supposed, in legend, to be a lost continent in the Atlantic Ocean, a paradise on earth whose people conquered all of southwestern Europe and northern Africa, but who were finally defeated by the Athenians. The people of Atlantis finally became wicked, so in punishment the island was swallowed up by the sea. Plato, the Greek philosopher, told this story in his work *Timaeus,* and even today, many people believe that Atlantis really existed.

HOW WERE MOUNTAINS MADE?

Mountains were formed millions of years ago, when the earth was settling down. Some mountains were begun when the earth was a ball of fire – like volcanoes, which are still burning, deep within the earth's crust. Others began with massive earthquakes, which forced and pushed the land together, forming great peaks when the land cooled and hardened. And some mountains happened because, as Earth spun round the sun, it became flatter at the North and South Poles, so the surface of the earth wrinkled, pushing up ridges and peaks which became mountains and mountain ranges.

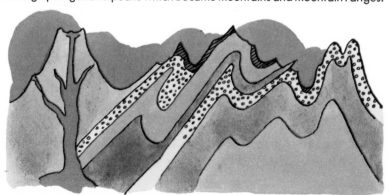

WHERE DID TEDDY BEARS COME FROM?

Teddy Bears began with the American President 'Teddy' Roosevelt, who was fond of hunting. One day he found a bear cub which had lost his mother and his kindness to the cub was noticed by a newspaper cartoonist. Afterwards Teddy Roosevelt went to a wedding and, at the reception, was given some toy bears. He was delighted and someone suggested they be called 'Teddy Bears', after Teddy Roosevelt. Soon toymakers were making a great many toy bears for children all over the world.

HOW DO CATS PURR?

A cat purrs when it feels happy or contented, and purring is caused by the vibrating of its vocal cords. When a cat takes air into its lungs, the air goes through the voice box that contains the vocal cords. Then if a cat feels happy, it will allow the cords to vibrate as air passes in and out. Other members of the cat family, such as the lion, tiger, jaguar and leopard cannot purr, because of a different formation of bones in the throat. The lion roars instead, and the jaguar and leopard make a noise like a hoarse bark.

WHO ARE THE GIPSIES?

Gipsies are bands of travelling peoples, who wander over the world without settling down and have their own customs and languages. Nobody knows for sure where gipsies originated, but they are believed to have come from India in the tenth century and migrated to Persia. They reached the Balkans and the Greek islands in the fourteenth century and, always moving west, reached Britain during the 1500s. Because they are different from those who have settled on the land or in towns they have always been disliked and hurried on from place to place. This attitude has encouraged the gipsies to keep to themselves and to keep their customs alive. Two tribes of gipsies are the Hungarian *tziganes*, and the Spanish *gitanos*. British people thought they came from Egypt, and called these people 'gipsies', but they call themselves 'Romanies' and their language 'Romany', and are a people proud of their past.

WHY DO WE CRY WHEN WE PEEL ONIONS?

We cry because of an oil called allyl which is inside every onion. When we cut into the onion, this oil escapes into the air and irritates the nerves in our eyes and nose. These nerves send a cry for help to the brain, and the brain responds with tears to soothe the stinging.

WHY DOES VENICE HAVE SO MANY CANALS?

The Italian city of Venice was built on a group of mud banks that formed many small islands at the head of the Adriatic Sea. No cars are allowed in the oldest parts of the city and people travel by boats or gondolas along the canals, which serve as streets. Venice began as twelve townships on the lagoon and this was the beginning of the state of Venice. Venice didn't become part of Italy until 1866, and this was because of a long and steady decline in power. In 1450, however, Venice had been the head of a large colonial empire and was the chief world sea-power.

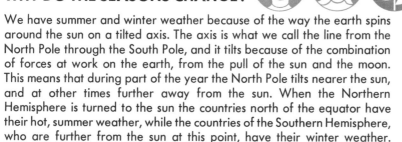

WHY DO THE SEASONS CHANGE?

We have summer and winter weather because of the way the earth spins around the sun on a tilted axis. The axis is what we call the line from the North Pole through the South Pole, and it tilts because of the combination of forces at work on the earth, from the pull of the sun and the moon. This means that during part of the year the North Pole tilts nearer the sun, and at other times further away from the sun. When the Northern Hemisphere is turned to the sun the countries north of the equator have their hot, summer weather, while the countries of the Southern Hemisphere, who are further from the sun at this point, have their winter weather.

WHY DO HUMMINGBIRDS HUM?

These small birds are very beautiful and can be found in dense jungles or by the sides of tropical mountains, mostly in Colombia and Equador. The humming noise they make is caused by the beating of their wings as they hover over the flowers where they gather nectar with long bills. The hummingbird's wings can beat up to seventy-five times in a single second, enabling the bird to reach speeds of fifty miles an hour! During the courtship flights of the humming-bird, its wings can beat as fast as two hundred times a second.

WHY DO WE SNEEZE?

Sneezing is a reflex action to expel air very quickly from the nose and mouth. We want to sneeze when our mucous membranes are irritated or swollen by a cold. During the sixth century there was a plague in Italy, so Pope Gregory the Great decided that prayers be said against sneezing, and this began the custom of saying 'God Bless You' after a sneeze.

WHAT WAS THE ALAMO?

The Alamo is a building in San Antonio, Texas. It was the chapel of a Franciscan mission in 1718, but by 1835 was sometimes used as a fort as the mission had long since left. In 1835 a band of American settlers in Texas – not yet part of the United States – revolted against the Mexicans, who at that time owned Texas. Davy Crockett came to help the American settlers and they took the Alamo building as their fort. Then the Mexican general, Antonio Lopez de Santa Anna, marched on San Antonio with 4,000 men. In the Alamo only 180 men waited, among them Colonel Travis and James Bowie. The Mexicans surrounded the fort, but the men in the Alamo held them back for thirteen days. Finally the Mexicans blasted a hole in the Alamo wall and got in that way. But as the Mexican troops poured into the old mission, the defenders of the Alamo went on fighting until every one of them was killed. The Mexicans were subsequently beaten in another battle during the next six months.

WHAT IS A "BLUE PETER"?

The "Blue Peter" is a blue flag with a white square in the centre. A ship always flies this flag when leaving port to sail. The flag stands for the letter P – for Peter – in the international code of signals.

DO YOU KNOW . . .
. . . THE MEANINGS OF THESE CATTY SAYINGS?

1. All cats love fish but fear to wet their paws.

This is said of anyone who is very keen to obtain something, but less keen to go to the necessary risk or trouble.

4. To be made a cat's paw of.

This means to be made to do another's dirty work for them, and is supposed to have originated in the story of a monkey who, wanting some chestnuts that were roasting in the fire, used the paw of his friend the cat to pull them out, rather than his own.

2. Before the cat can lick her ear.

This means 'never', since no cat could ever manage to lick its ear.

3. To fight like Kilkenny cats.

This means to fight very determinedly until completely exhausted. It is said that when the town of Kilkenny was occupied by troops during the 1798 Irish rebellion, some soldiers amused themselves by tying two cats together and throwing them over a clothes-line to fight. When an officer came to see what was going on, a soldier hurriedly cut the cats free by severing their tails. The explanation given for the two bleeding tails on the line was that the cats, in fighting, had devoured each other all but the tails.

5. Who is to bell the cat?

This means: who will risk his life to save another's? Again the source is an old fable, on this occasion the story of an old mouse who suggested a bell was hung on the cat's neck to warn of its approach. This was fine, said a wise young mouse, but who was to undertake the job of attaching the bell?

. . . AND OF THESE FELINE EXPRESSIONS?

1. Cat's cradle.

This is a string game for two, popular with children. It is thought the name might come from the word 'cratch-cradle', meaning a manger of the sort in which Jesus was laid. 'Cratch' comes from the French word for cradle, which is 'crèche'.

2. Cat's eyes.

These are reflectors which are positioned along our roads to help drivers when it is dark. The name clearly comes from the fact that all that can be seen of a cat in the dark is its large gleaming eyes.

3. The cat's pyjamas.

This means 'the best' or 'first-rate', and was originally an American expression. 'The cat's whiskers' is used in the same way, and has the same meaning.

4. Cat's whisker.

This was the name given to the fine wire in a 'crystal' wireless set that actually made contact with the crystal.

FACT OR FICTION?

Many popular beliefs about animals are taken for granted, but are they actually based on the true facts?

An elephant never forgets

Surprisingly this belief does have some truth in it. Experiments have shown that, having been taught a series of tests, an elephant is capable of remembering more than three quarters of them a year later. Elephants, while extremely slow learners, undoubtedly do have good memories.

Red rags enrage bulls

This belief is something of a non-starter since bulls, like most mammals—with the exception of men and monkeys—are colour blind. Although matadors traditionally use red cloaks—perhaps to hide the bloodstains—other colours make bulls angry just as effectively. It is the **movement** of the cloak, rather than its being red, that enrages bulls.

Rats desert a sinking ship

It has long been thought that rats possess a prophetic power, capable of foreseeing the sinking of a ship. Useful a sign though this would be, rats, like humans, only desert ships when the water rises inside and threatens to drown them. Since rats generally live in the holds of ships they would doubtless have an early warning, but this would be based on sea water rather than a sixth sense.

Music charms snakes

Believe this at your peril! Snakes are in fact deaf, having no ears, but they respond to the rhythmic vibrations of a charmer's foot tapping the ground and the swaying of his body and pipe.

ASKING ABOUT ANIMALS

1. What is an accentor?

2. Where are penguins found, the Arctic, the Antarctic, or both?

3. What is a briard?

4. Some animals sleep right through the cold winter months. What is this long sleep called?

5. Which is the only bear still found in South America?

6. What is the smallest breed of dog?

7. What type of creature is the hammerhead?

8. One way to tell the difference between Indian and African elephants is to compare the size of their ears. Which has the larger ears?

9. Where did the golden hamster, now popular as a pet, originate?

10. What does the word hamster mean?

Answers

1. It is a bird, widespread in Europe, and related to the dunnock; 2. The Antarctic; 3. A sheepdog, particularly popular in France; 4. Hibernation; 5. The Andean or spectacled bear, so-called for its distinctive facial markings; 6. The chihuahua, usually about 7" high; 7. A shark; 8. The African elephant; 9. Syria; 10. In German the word means 'hoarder', very apt for this small animal, which stores large amounts of food.

LAST WORDS
Which famous people had these as their last words?

1. "Die, my dear doctor?
That's the last thing I shall do."

2. "Kiss me, Hardy."

3. "Is that you, Dora?"

4. "Qualis artifex pereo."
(What an artist the world is losing in me.)

5. "Treason! Treason!"

6. "Light, more light!"

IS IT TRUE THAT . . .

. . . Birds Hibernate?

Certain birds do hibernate, one of them being the poor-will, which is found in the western parts of the United States. In the 1940s a scientist found a poor-will in a torpid state and ringed it. He found that the bird returned to the same place in successive winters and slept until spring; it hibernated. How is it able to survive? When they are not active the body working slows down, as does the body temperature, so that a little stored fat will provide enough energy to keep the bird alive until spring (and a fresh food supply) comes. Poor-wills are rarely seen, being nocturnal in habit, and equipped with very effective camouflage markings. They feed on moths and beetles, flying with their beaks wide open, scooping up food as they go. During the day they sleep among rocks, for they do not make nests, laying their eggs in a simple scrape in the ground.

. . . Millipedes Really Have 1,000 Legs?

Although millipedes hold the world record for the largest number of feet, it is unlikely that any have as many as 1,000. Moulting occurs regularly throughout a millipede's life, and after each moult an extra body segment grows, complete with two pairs of feet, so that as it grows older a millipede grows longer and longer, and has more and more pairs of feet! Although a millipede's many feet are well co-ordinated, it does not move quickly, and is only active at night, spending its days hiding in the soil or under stones, feeding on dead leaves and plants that grow in damp places. There are hundreds of species of millipede, most of them to be found in Africa, though the largest is to be found in the Seychelles. It grows to 12″ in length!

. . . Moles Are Blind?

Moles are not completely blind, though their eyesight is very poor. This is because they spend almost all their time underground, only venturing above the ground at night. For this reason their eyes have become somewhat unnecessary, the tiny eyes being almost hidden by fur. The mole digs a series of underground tunnels and corridors, and runs along them, sniffing out its food of worms, insects and other small creatures. Its appetite is enormous—it eats its own body weight in food every day. Imagine a 10 stone man eating 10 stones of food every day!

. . . The Upside-Down Catfish Swims Upside-Down?

The upside-down catfish can swim normally or on its back. It usually swims upside-down so that it can feed on the surface of the water more easily. Even the fish's colouration is adapted: it has a dark belly and a light back, the opposite of a normal fish's camouflage system.

. . . Hedgehogs Are Found in the Desert?

Certain species of hedgehog are able to live in desert areas. They resemble our own common hedgehog, but are much smaller, growing to a length of between 6 and 9 inches. Found in the dry, arid areas of Africa and Asia, the desert hedgehog spends most of the daylight hours in a hole dug in the ground so that it is reasonably cool, emerging at night to go in search of food—insects. The hedgehog is remarkably well adapted to the harsh desert life, being able to survive for more than two months without food or water.

SNAKES ALIVE!

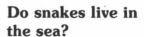

Is the blind snake really blind?

Blind snakes live underground and are practically blind, though perfectly suited to their subterranean existence, being smooth, shiny and slender so that they move easily through the ground. The heads are bony, unlike other snakes, so that they can excavate tunnels with them. There are many species, none growing much longer than about 7″.

Do snakes live in the sea?

Many snakes have adopted aquatic habits, and are never seen on dry land. One of them, the tentacled snake, is often found in fishing nets on the coast of Thailand. It is not a true sea snake, but nevertheless is never seen on dry land, feeding on small fishes, molluscs and crustaceans. The two tentacle-like growths on the snout give it its name. The function of these growths is not known, though some scientists believe that they may have something to do with the detection of prey.

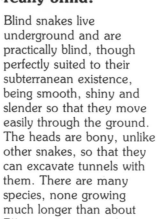

How did the boomslang get its name?

Boomslang is the Afrikaans word for 'tree snake'. Found in southern Africa, it lives in the trees, climbing swiftly and nimbly. It eats small reptiles, animals and birds, and will steal eggs and young birds from nests, killing its prey with very powerful venom.

Which is the longest and heaviest of all snakes?

That record goes to the anaconda of South America. They spend most of their time immersed in water, and feed on small deer and other mammals, strangling their prey by coiling around it, then opening their huge and flexible jaws and swallowing the animal whole. Anacondas longer than 20′are quite common, though there have been claims of snakes as long as 40′. One snake shot in the Orinoco River was measured at 37½′, but before it could be authenticated, the snake recovered and escaped!

LANGUAGES OF THE WORLD

What alphabet is used by deaf people?

Understanding what somebody else is saying when you are deaf can be an impossible task, making the deaf person feel isolated and alone. Dumb people, unable to speak, are similarly denied the basic human medium of communication. **Finger spelling** is a method of talking to someone using a signalling code, similar to semaphore. The two-handed method used in Australia, Britain, Burma, India and some other countries, utilises relative positions of the hands and fingers to spell different letters. It is quicker to learn than the one-handed method and can be seen more clearly at a distance.

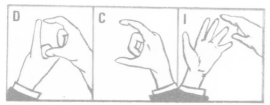

Which European language has the largest vocabulary?

The **English** language is spoken by approximately 400 million people, making it the second most-used language on Earth, though it is generally agreed that it is the richest of the world's 5,000 languages. Four hundred years ago English was spoken only by the inhabitants of the British Isles, but today more than half the world's magazines, newspapers and scientific journals are printed in English.

In 1066 the language only had a vocabulary of about 30,000 words, whereas modern English is estimated to include some 500,000 words, of which only 200,000 are in current use. An average person today knows and uses at least 10,000 words and can understand a conversation of up to 322 words a minute. In conversation the word 'I' is most used, while in writing it is 'the'.

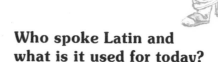

Who spoke Latin and what is it used for today?

Latin was originally spoken by people living in and around Rome, taking its name from one of the tribes living in the Tiber Valley, the *Latini*. The Latin that is used or studied today comes from a period several hundred years later, by which time it had become a refined and dignified language used mainly by educated Romans, such as administrators, orators and writers. A more vulgar version was used by the uneducated masses.

Latin was the principle language of Europe for hundreds of years, and its influence on modern European languages is immense, although it has not been in general use itself since the Middle Ages. Latin is widely used for scientific and legal terminology.

Which language is spoken by most people?

Over 500 million people speak one of the **Mandarin Chinese** dialects. Chinese is unlike most other languages as it has no alphabet, but uses instead several thousand *characters* or symbols, each of which conveys one complete idea. Each *character* has only one syllable, and most words are made up of two or more characters. A character can change its meaning by the way it is pronounced or by changing its position in a sentence. It is only in the last hundred years that ways have been invented to write Chinese in the Roman alphabet.

CANALS

The Canals of Britain

It's quite likely that you live quite near to a canal – though you might not know it. Even today, a huge complex of canals criss-crosses Britain, although many of them are overgrown now. But once canals were the backbone of Britain's prosperity, carrying goods of all kinds from place to place efficiently and quickly. The tragedy is that these canals were allowed to decline when roads and railways developed, so that now the country owns many stretches of canals with little or no use – they're too old and decayed. Recently new interest has been shown, however, with teams of young workers renovating the canals and people holidaying in barges, seeing from a new angle the incomparable beauty of the countryside – from the canals!

It all began in 1761 with the opening of the Bridgewater canal in Lancashire. This was the brainchild of the Duke of Bridgewater and it nearly bankrupted him; but after its opening the canal began to recoup the Duke's investment handsomely. The engineer was James Brindley, whose genius was to make the canal system such a success. In fact, the Bridgewater canal was so profitable that in the next seventy years some 5,000 miles of waterways were opened. It wasn't until Thomas Telford brought his brilliant mind to work, though, that canals stopped following the sometimes extremely tortuous contours of the land, in favour of aqueducts and embankments.

During this reckless boom time of canal-building, many fortunes were won and lost, but despite the

TELFORD

adventures and the disasters, Britain was left with a system of inland waterways which covered just about every area of the country. It was during the nineteenth century that the canals reached their peak of success, and were largely responsible for the industrial greatness Britain enjoyed at that time. Unfortunately railways came with progress and proved to be a far more dangerous rival than the inconvenient roads had been. It wasn't only their speed, it was also the practice of the railways to buy up stretches of canals only to let them run down, that finally brought the canal system to its knees.

Nowadays there are still boats on the canals – and some do carry freight, but the general atmosphere is one of dereliction. Narrow boats, carrying goods,

usually travel in pairs – the 'motor boat' and the 'butty', and between them can carry up to fifty tons. There are still the gaily-painted traditional narrow boats which are lived in all the year round by families who have made the canals their life; and who can blame them, for they see much more of the unspoiled, peaceful scenery than car and rail-travellers are ever likely to see!

The situation does seem more hopeful, however, with the work of the Inland Waterways Association and its efforts to get many canals open for public use again – and succeeding! One of their most spectacular feats was the clearing of sixteen miles (on which stood thirty-six locks) of the Stratford-on-Avon canal, which had been virtually derelict since 1930.

Canals to visit are the Staffordshire and Worcestershire canal, especially at Caldwell Lock, near Kidderminster – the surroundings here are really picturesque – and the Grand Union canal at Wolverton, where you can see an aqueduct standing thirty-five feet above the River Ouse. This was built in 1811, and is still in use!

Canals are still a way of life for many people. Anglers use the waterways regularly, and there are reputedly more than three million of them! Apart from this, canals are often a relief from city landscapes – even the dilapidated ones! – for walking the dog or just taking some air. It does seem a shame that these invaluable amenities couldn't be repaired completely; the advantages would be enormous, for both industry and recreation.

PHOTO FILE

J.N. Niepce

W.H. Fox Talbot

Who invented Photography and when?

There was no single 'inventor' of photography. It *evolved* through the combined work of many people of many different nationalities.

One Frenchman, Joseph Nicephore Niepce (1765–1833), often gets the credit, however, since he was the first to obtain a picture 'from nature' with a camera, in the modern photographic sense. He was also the first to 'fix' a picture, so that it did not immediately deteriorate, though the result was still not as permanent as with a present-day 'fixer'.

A plaque near the estate where Niepce used to live reads: "Dans ce village Nicephore Niepce inventa la Photographie en 1822". Experts, having examined the metal plate used in this first photograph, think 1826 is probably more accurate.

It was in 1839, when the painter Jacques Daguerre's process was made public, that the subject of photography became known. Daguerre had modified Niepce's work to produce his daguerreotype. It was recorded that "opticians' shops were crowded with amateurs panting for daguerreotype apparatus, and . . . everyone wanted to record the view from his window."

Who coined the term Photography and what does it mean?

The word was coined by the astronomer, Sir John Herschel, in 1839, and replaced the term 'Photogenic Drawing' used by William Talbot, an English amateur scientist who had been experimenting along his own lines, parallel to Daguerre.

'Photography' is from the Greek: Photos (light) + graphos (writing). It therefore means 'writing with light'.

Herschel also coined the terms 'negative' and 'positive', as the two stages in producing a photograph. His friend Talbot was the first person to reverse negative photograms – photographs made without a camera, by simply laying objects on a piece of photographic paper and exposing the paper to light – to obtain a positive picture on a second sheet of light-sensitized paper.

Daguerre's apparatus

L.J.M. Daguerre

How was the word camera derived and what are or were: (a) camera obscura; (b) camera lucida; (c) detective cameras; (d) candid cameras?

'Camera' is again from the Greek: 'kamara', meaning 'anything with an arched cover'. In fact, in later cameras this was superceded by a box structure – basically a light-tight box with a light-sensitive film at one end, and a lens or pinhole at the other. It is fairly simple to make a pinhole camera, but nowadays most cameras are a lot more sophisticated.

(a) *camera obscura* is an apparatus which projects an image of a distant object onto a wall or screen. The term means 'dark-room'. It was used by artists in Renaissance times and at first, light was introduced simply by a hole in a wall. Then in 1550, a lens was introduced. The image projected was always inverted.

Camera Obscura

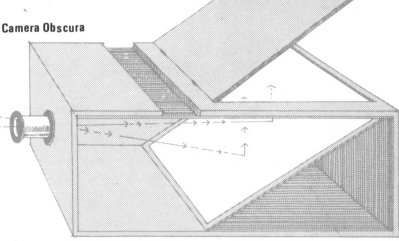

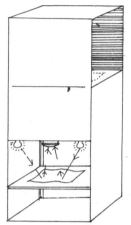

(b) *camera lucida* is the term for a Light Box (its other name) invented by Natan Lerner. The box should be at least four feet long, three feet wide and two feet high, and the bigger the better.

One side is open and the inside is painted black. A camera lens is inserted into a central hole at one end, and objects can be placed over, or spotlights shone through, other holes at the sides of the box.

Tobacco smoke, for instance, can be puffed in to produce shafts of light, enabling one to photograph light in purer form; and light can be directed and filtered to obtain different desired lighting effects and moods.

The Light Box was also used by artists.

(c) *detective cameras* (early hand cameras) were so called because 'surreptitious' shots could be taken with them. This was because of the size of them. They became a craze, and were often disguised as paper parcels or pieces of luggage, or hidden in people's hats.

One of the first commercial makes of camera was George Eastman's first Kodak box camera in 1888.

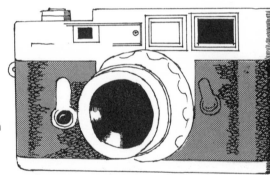

Leica

An early detective camera

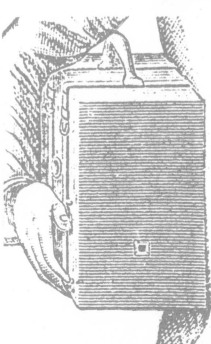

(d) *candid cameras* were so called because (using only available light – i.e. no flashlight) they could take pictures *indoors* without the subject knowing his picture was being taken.

This development was made possible by the improved quality of lenses in the 1920s, meaning 'what you could see you could photograph'.

The Leica was the first candid or *miniature* camera, in 1924, and it was also the first to use 35mm film.

The detective camera, and now the candid camera, were the earliest examples of recording moments of 'life passing by', which is the basis of modern photo-journalism.

STRANGE-SOUNDING SPORTS

What sort of sport was Savate?

It was a French form of kick boxing, popular in the 18th century. It has now died out, but contributed much to the style of French boxing now being revived as one of the modern martial arts.

What is Shorinji-kempo?

This is one of the most popular Japanese martial arts, with around a million people practising the sport. Over 2,000 years old, it was originally introduced into China by a Buddhist monk from India.

The uniform for the sport is the traditional black robe of the Chinese monks, and although there are superficial similarities with ju-jitsu, with similar holds and throws being used, Shorinji-kempo has an emphasis on balancing the active side with the calm of meditation.

What equipment is used in Skiyaking?

To skiyak, you need two narrow, elongated boats (like kayaks) which are worn like skis. There is an opening for each foot rather like an air-filled pocket, and these pockets help to keep you stable.

The idea is to push forwards with each foot alternately, getting up speed with the aid of a double-bladed paddle. On running water with a favourable current, it is possible to reach 30 mph.

The skiyaks are made of polyester resin, and are unsinkable.

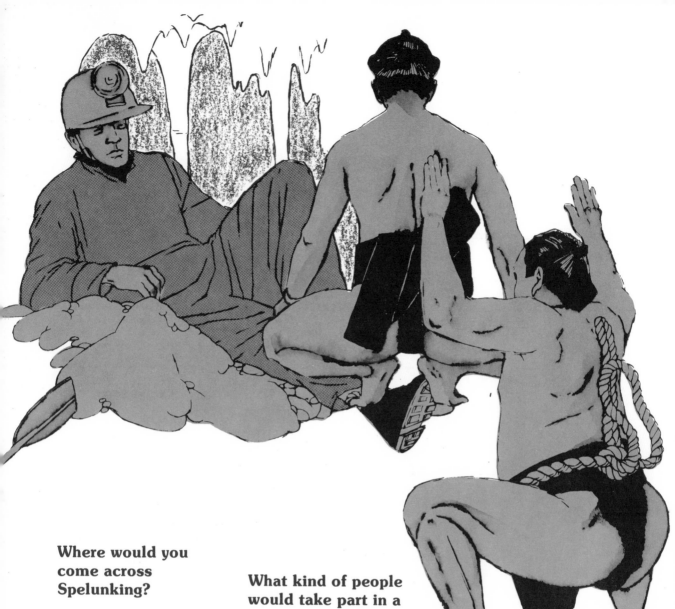

Where would you come across Spelunking?

In caves, for this is another name for caving, coming from the old English word 'spelunk' (meaning cave).

This is a non-competitive sport, taken up for fun and for the enjoyment of the natural underground beauty of the caves. However, it can be dangerous and should always be done in groups. Proper equipment is essential, especially sturdy boots, warm and waterproof clothing (caves are often damp and chilly even in summer), lights, ropes, a first-aid kit and food.

What kind of people would take part in a bout of Sumo?

Most likely huge Japanese men, weighing as much as 25 stone, for Sumo is the traditional form of Japanese wrestling and, as far as its fans are concerned, the larger the contestants the better!

At the beginning of a bout, the wrestlers spend a few minutes alternately throwing salt (a special ritual), stomping, squatting and glaring at each other. Then, when physical contact begins, the aim is to drive the opponent out of the ring, or to throw him to the ground.

Although Sumo is one of the most popular Japanese sports, it is largely a spectator sport, with less than 1,000 active participants. Wrestlers are often recruited as young as twelve years old, and then housed in a sort of monastery where they undergo intensive training while serving their elders.

PEOPLE AND PLACES

What was Tasmania originally called?

This island, lying off the coast of Southern Australia, was discovered by a Dutchman, Abel Tasman, in 1642. Sent by the governor of the Dutch East Indies (present-day Indonesia), Tasman first called the island **Van Diemen's Land** in his honour, and sent the ship's carpenter to swim ashore and erect a pole claiming the place for the Dutch East India Company. It was the British who renamed the island Tasmania in 1885. Regrettably, European settlers—including many convicts—succeeded in causing the deaths of every last native aborigine on the island by 1876.

What Country, discovered by a NORWEGIAN, was named by a GERMAN after an ITALIAN?

It was an odd chance of fate that neither of the two disputed discoverers of America, Leif Ericson or Christopher Columbus, gave his name to the new continent. The *Italian* geographer, **Amerigo Vespucci,** commanding two *Spanish* ships under the *Portuguese* flag, explored in detail a considerable stretch of the east coast of South America between 1497 and 1501. He described the continent as 'a new world', and this term so inspired the *German* publisher Waldseemuller, that when he produced a world map in 1507 he labelled the southern land mass **'America'.** Once it became clear that the northern and southern land masses were one continent, the whole of it became known as America.

Which African State has had three names within the last twenty years?

For the last seventy years this country in Southern Africa was called **Southern Rhodesia;** when Northern Rhodesia became Zambia in 1964, it resorted simply to **Rhodesia,** as it had been known when Cecil Rhodes, the British colonial statesman, had originally united the Matabele and Mashona tribes under one colony. With the introduction of the first modern black government in 1979, however, the country was renamed **Zimbabwe Rhodesia,** after a well-organised and flourishing African civilisation which ruled Rhodesia more than 1,000 years ago. The first black president, Josiah Gumede, is an ancestor of Chaka, the legendary 19th century Zulu chief.

Which Middle Eastern State is named after a Biblical Character?

The state of **Israel** was established in 1948. In Biblical times the leader of the Jewish faith, Abraham, settled his followers in Palestine. They belonged to a group of tribes known as the Hebrews, who are sometimes called Israelites, because Jacob, Abraham's son, is said by the Old Testament to have been given the name **Israel** by God. Many Jews fled from Palestine because of persecution by the Romans, but in the late nineteenth century Jewish settlers returned to live in Palestine, and this led to the creation of modern Israel.

WHO WAS PILTDOWN MAN?

Piltdown Man was said to be proof of the missing link in the evolutionary chain, bridging the gap between ape and man — or was he?

One day in 1908 amateur archaeologist Charles Dawson was walking on Piltdown Common, just outside the village of Fletching in Sussex, England. Always on the lookout for interesting fossils, he noticed workmen digging in a gravel bed, moving gravel that evidently dated from the early Ice Age. He urged them to watch for anything unusual, and was delighted when they reported finding a piece of skull. Dawson and other diggers found more pieces of skull in the years that followed, as well as flint and bone tools, animal bones and teeth, and an ape-like jawbone. They were all found in the early Ice Age level of the gravel, and Dawson naturally supposed that the bones dated from that time.

Were the bones authentic?

One person who believed so was Sir Arthur Smith Woodward, Keeper of the Department of Geology at the British Museum, and a friend of Dawson's. He was very excited by the find, and in 1912 announced to the world that the skull and jawbone were from the same creature, the 'missing link' between ape and man. Piltdown Man became famous, for most people believed that the bones were the earliest ever discovered, and lengthy papers and books were written on the subject. Sir Arthur gave many lectures, backed up by an artist's impression of the Piltdown Man, hairy, with a flat nose, low brow and chinless jaw. Though some experts doubted the authenticity of the bones, they were definitely in a small minority, and for the next forty years Piltdown Man was accepted as genuine.

How were the bones proved to be fake, after all?

It wasn't until after the Second World War that a new method for testing the age of fossils was discovered. Based on the idea that anything which lies in the ground absorbs fluorine from water, and that the older that thing is the more it will contain, scientists could date fossils quite accurately. The Piltdown bones were subjected to the tests, and a dumbfounded world learned that they were fakes. Further tests, using the Carbon-14 method, confirmed the facts.

But how were the bones faked?

The pieces of skull were human, but they were only a few thousand years old. The jawbone was not that of the so-called Piltdown Man, but that of an ape, crudely stained so that it looked much older, and matched the skull. And the animal bones and teeth? One proved to be a fossilised elephant tooth from Tunisia; another a hippopotamus tooth from Malta! Even the flint tools were found to have been given an appearance of age, and the bone tool (which had been considered unique) was found to have been shaped with a modern tool.

Who faked the Piltdown Man?

That is something which remains a mystery to this day. Piltdown Man was a gigantic — and very successful — hoax, but as to who perpetrated that hoax, we do not know. Only one thing is certain — the so-called 'Piltdown Man', the missing link in the evolutionary chain — never existed.

THE ROYAL MAIL

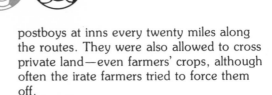

Every time you post a letter, it is carried by the Royal Mail. But has this always been true?

The answer is no—the original Royal Posts were only used for state business, and other letter-writers (then mainly monks, scholars and merchants) had to make their own arrangements.

Messengers were used to deliver the king's letters as long ago as the Middle Ages. They rode on horseback, and were chosen for their speed, honesty and bravery. Not only did they have to get the mail delivered quickly, they also had to protect it from frequent attacks by highwaymen.

In the sixteenth century the messengers began to carry private letters, and they were given uniforms and called 'postboys'. Then, from 1609 onwards, all post had to be carried by the Royal Mail.

Unfortunately, the roads at this time were atrocious, so fresh horses were kept for the postboys at inns every twenty miles along the routes. They were also allowed to cross private land—even farmers' crops, although often the irate farmers tried to force them off.

As more people learnt to write, and the volume of post increased, letters were carried in mail-bags, and delivered to post-inns around the country. In a way these were the forerunners of our post offices, just as the postboys preceded our postmen, and the mail-coaches preceded our Royal Mail vans and travelling post-offices.

The first mail-coach ran in 1784, from Bristol to London, and within twenty years there were two hundred coaches, running to a timetable, and each carrying an armed guard.

They had 'Royal Mail' painted on their sides, just as the mail trains did when they were introduced in Victorian times, and just as the fleet of about 26,000 Post Office vans do today.

What was the first postage stamp? When were the first charges made for delivering letters? When and where was the first pillar-box erected?

The first postage stamp was the *Penny Black*, showing the head of Queen Victoria, the reigning monarch of the time. It was issued in 1840 and, as its name suggests, cost one penny.

The first charges for delivering letters were made in 1708, when a halfpenny post began in London. This was before both stamps and pillar-boxes, and postmen called *letter carriers* walked through the streets to collect the letters and the halfpennies. They used to ring a bell to let people know they were coming.

So much for the past, but what happens to a letter you post now?

It wasn't until 1855 that the first pillar-box was put up. This is what it looked like. It was on the corner of Farringdon Street and Fleet Street, in London. As you can see, it was 5 furlongs 213 yards from the General Post Office— and to give you an idea how far that is, there were 8 furlongs in a mile (one furlong = 220 yards).

This is the sort of pillar-box we have now, and unless you happen to post your letter at a Post Office, this will be the beginning of its journey. A plate on the front of the box gives the times at which a van will come to collect the mail.

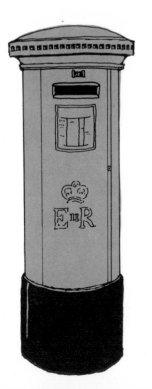

The mail bags are taken to the local *sorting office*, unloaded from the van, and put on a *chain conveyor*, which takes them off up to the sorting machinery.

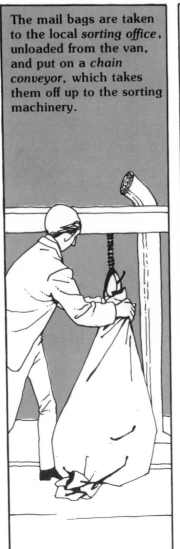

The first machine is called a *segregator*, and has a moving belt onto which the contents of the bags are tipped. It then separates letters from packets, and bigger envelopes from smaller ones.

When they have been sorted by size, the next step involves the stamp, and is carried out by a machine called ALF. This stands for *automatic letter facer,* and ALF's first task is to arrange all the letters so that their stamps are in the top right-hand corner, a job known as *facing.*

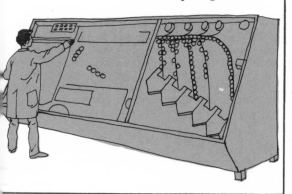

ALF also sorts first-class from second-class mail, by 'reading' the different phosphor bands running through each stamp. You can just see these bands if you look at a stamp in the right light—enough at least to see the different bands on first and second class stamps.

When ALF has turned all the letters the right way round, it puts a postmark on each stamp, so that it cannot be used again. This is called *cancelling.* Each postmark indicates where and when the letter was posted.

Letters then used to be sorted by hand, into the pigeon holes corresponding to the various areas of delivery, whether towns or rural districts, in this country or abroad. But in the most up-to-date sorting offices, this stage is now semi-automated, using *coding desks* attached to an *automatic letter sorter.*

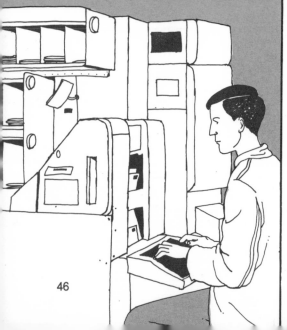

A man sits at each desk and operates a keyboard, instructing the machine to put coded phosphor dots onto each letter, corresponding to the *postcode* on the envelope. Although we cannot see them, these dots are 'read' by the sorting machine, which sends each letter into its correct pigeon hole.

The operation will only become fully automatic when some way is found for people to write onto an envelope something which a machine can understand, without need for coding in between.

Letters for each destination are now bundled together and bagged, ready for the next stage of the journey. This may only be a local delivery, in which case it would only involve one postman, or possibly a short trip by van.

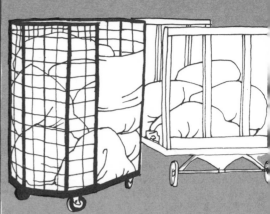

For longer journeys, mail usually goes by train, during the night, arriving very early the next morning. Some mail goes by ordinary passenger trains, but at night there are special mail trains, known as *travelling-post-offices*. Letters can be sorted en route, to save time on arrival.

Letters going abroad travel either by sea or by air. Air mail is quicker, but also more expensive— except to nearer countries on the Continent, where all mail goes by air.

Sometimes inland mail goes by road, for instance in rural areas where there is no railway. In the heart of London, however, the traffic is often very slow-moving, so the Post Office has its own underground railway, with ten kilometres of track linking six main sorting offices and two of the main line railway stations.

One way or another, the mail bags eventually reach the sorting office at the far end, where letters are to be sorted into the various local delivery areas. This operation, known as *setting in,* is traditionally the job of the early morning sorter.

However, today sorting machines can use the second half of the postcodes, again by reading the phosphor dots, to sort out the mail street-by-street. (If the postcode were AX1 4WA, the first half denotes the larger area, Axborough— the rest locates the street). This was a job the postman originally did himself before setting out on his round.

The postman is dropped off by van at the beginning of his *walk*. This is the name for the patch one postman covers, and the specific route he takes. In fact, not all postmen walk—some ride bicycles and others drive vans (where larger distances are to be covered, especially in the country).

When your letter pops through the door in the morning, its journey is over, along with millions of others delivered that day. There are nearly 100,000 postmen who deliver letters to 20 million addresses in Britain, and if all the letters posted in one day were placed on top of one another, the pile would be four times the height of Mount Everest!

HOW IT WORKS

Thermostat

This is a device to control temperature automatically, and is usually made of two different metals joined together to form a strip.

One metal expands more than the other when heated, so, as the temperature rises, the metal that expands more lengthens and pushes the strip into a curve.

The curve moves away from an electric contact, and by doing this, switches off the supply of electricity. Then, as the metal cools, the strip straightens, so that it touches the contact again, and switches on the current.

Hence the thermostat switches *off* the electricity when it is too hot, and *on* again when too cold, thus keeping the temperature between the two set limits.

Thermostats are often used in electric irons, cookers and radiators.

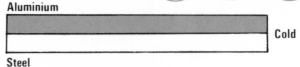

Aluminium

Steel

Cold

Hot

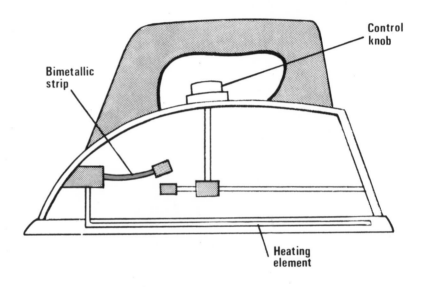

Control knob

Bimetallic strip

Heating element

Thermos (Flask)

This works using a vacuum. Indeed it is also known as a *vacuum flask* — or sometimes a Dewar flask after the British scientist, Sir James Dewar, who invented it in the 1880s.

The name *Thermos* was the trade name under which the flasks were first sold.

It consists of one glass vessel, sealed inside another. The air between the two has been removed to form the vacuum. A cork closes the mouth of the flask, and there is an outer metal case to protect the glass from damage.

Glass, cork and the vacuum are all bad conductors of heat, i.e. heat passes through them very slowly. On top of this, the glass surfaces are polished (silvered) to make them even worse radiators of heat.

Hence these flasks are able to keep at a constant temperature for some length of time, and they are used to keep cold liquids cold, or hot liquids hot.

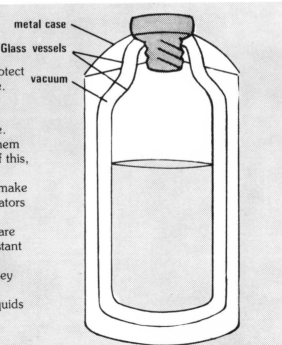

metal case

Glass vessels

vacuum

WHO WAS REMBRANDT?

Rembrandt Harmensz van Rijn was one of the greatest artists in the world. Born in 1606 in the town of Leyden, Holland, he created three hundred etchings, more than two thousand drawings and over six hundred paintings, many of which are priceless masterpieces.

Rembrandt's father was a miller. After being sent to university in Leyden at fourteen, Rembrandt decided he would become a painter and practised working on canvases at home, using his brothers and sisters as models. Then he was sent to Amsterdam where he studied under Pieter Lastman, a gifted artist who had travelled in Italy and was influenced by Tintoretto. Lastman himself had a strong influence on Rembrandt's early work.

In 1625, a young man, Rembrandt returned to Leyden determined to make a career for himself there. He was such a success in his home town that he was encouraged to return to the capital, Amsterdam, and settled there permanently in 1631.

Two years later Rembrandt married Saskia van Uijlenburgh, daughter of an art dealer, who appeared in countless etchings and paintings during their happy years together. It was during this time that Rembrandt became more widely known in wealthy Amsterdam circles, and seemed set to enjoy a prosperous life as an artist. His direct, uncomplicated style with subtle overtones, and imaginative use of light and shadow, made his work as admired then as it is now. It was his interest in, and deep understanding of the people he portrayed that gave his work such honesty. Among his many subjects he was fond of religious themes, and there are also the self-portraits he painted throughout his life – valuable in themselves for the light they throw upon the changing fortunes of Rembrandt's life, since the artist left little or no written information about himself.

Life did not continue so successfully as before: with the completion of perhaps his best-

known work, the *Night Watch*, Rembrandt's fame paradoxically declined. Saskia died, the painting received savage criticism, and he was soon close to bankruptcy.

Throughout all this he was still a painter, and the work produced during this period, including the famous self-portrait of 1656, mirrored his misfortunes, adding greater depths and majesty to his masterpieces. In 1656 he did in fact go bankrupt, and spent the last decade of his life in poverty, but he still continued painting until his death in 1669. Some of his best works were completed towards the end of his life, and now his paintings hang in art galleries and private collections all over the world.

Which tree is favoured for making the best woodwind instruments?

The laburnum. This tree, with its lovely hanging blossoms and delicate leaves, has heartwood (the wood below the bark which you can see) of a rich, dark-brown colour which is exceptionally stable and dense, with good resonance, too. Not thick enough to be used for construction purposes, laburnum wood is used to make flutes, oboes and the chanters and drones for bagpipes.

Which tree's name arises from confusion with another tree in the Bible, whose fruits enabled John the Baptist to survive in the wilderness?

The locust, a tree native to eastern North America. The pale grey bark is very rough and the tree has attractive chains of blossom rather similar to the sweet pea flower during June. The wood is used for good furniture. The locust has hard, black peas in pods which the early settlers in America confused with the sweet fruits of the real locust tree.

Which tree is almost always found near water?

The alder. It grows by the sides of rivers and lakes, or beside a water source which has since dried up. Its tiny seeds have 'wings' to make them water-borne and will only sprout in damp mud. The roots like swampy soil and the leaf-fall enriches the land. The alder has a dark-grey or black bark, deeply cracked and fissured, and rich green, tooth-edged leaves. The cones, the alder's most distinctive feature, bear the seeds which float away on the water to take root elsewhere.

Which tree's berries are used to flavour gin and can be used in cookery?

The juniper. This evergreen tree is small and resembles a gorse bush with its spiky needles and fragrant grey bark. Juniper wood is used for small decorative carving and inlay, but it is the berries which make it useful. These are distilled into oil of juniper, which is then used in perfumery and exotic cookery. Another of its uses was in medicine, but nowadays its main function is to flavour gin.

Which tree's name derives from the old Norse word *ron* and the Gaelic *rhuadan*, and why?

The rowan. These words both mean red and describe the rowan's distinctive scarlet berries. The rowan grows on mountains and in highland regions, and is a small, sturdy tree with attractive feathery leaves. Rowan trees are believed to be lucky and were planted to keep witches away. Their berries are too acid to be eaten raw, but make delicious jellies.

POETS' CORNER

Both Shelley and Byron were poets of the Romantic age, geniuses of their time. Even today their poetry is read and appreciated by people all over the world. They led fascinating lives. . . .

Percy Bysshe Shelley

Shelley was born in Sussex in 1792, and grew up an imaginative boy living in his own world of make-believe and drama, until he was sent away to Eton in 1804. There he experienced unmerciful bullying which left its mark on his temperament, although he was a good student, if a little unconventional.

He went on to University College, Oxford, but was expelled from there after only five months for publishing *The Necessity of Atheism*. He went to live in London and would not be reconciled with his father, although his sisters visited him. And it was through them that he met Harriet Westbrook, who was then only fifteen.

Before the end of that year, he and Harriet had eloped to Edinburgh and been married. For two years they were very happy, travelling around Britain, and Shelley wrote his first important poem, *Queen Mab*. In 1813 Harriet bore a daughter, whom they called Ianthe, after the heroine in *Queen Mab*.

Soon, however, Shelley met Mary Godwin, the daughter of William Godwin, whose books had inspired Shelley at Eton. Soon he and Mary were deeply in love, and in 1814 they escaped to France, but returned after six weeks to find that Harriet had spent all Shelley's money. It was only the death of Shelley's father which kept them solvent, and after settling on an allowance, Harriet agreed to be separated from Shelley.

Mary and Shelley travelled on the Continent, after the publication of a new poem, *Alastor*, and met Byron there. Mary also wrote a story that won her lasting fame – *Frankenstein*.

Harriet drowned herself in 1816, and Shelley married Mary Godwin soon afterwards. Two years later they went back to Italy, and the Shelleys became close friends of Byron. It was during the last five years of his life that Shelley produced his best poetry, and while he was in Italy he wrote *Prometheus Unbound*, *The Cloud*, *The Skylark* and *Ode to the West Wind*. Learning of Keats' death in 1821 he wrote *Adonais* in memory of him.

Only a year later, Shelley was drowned when his boat was caught in a storm in the bay of Spezia, near Leghorn. His body was recovered ten days later, and friends, including Byron, built a funeral pyre on the beach. Byron couldn't bear to watch and leapt into the sea, to swim to his boat. Shelley's tomb is now in Rome, engraved with the words:

> *"Nothing of him that doth fade,*
> *But doth suffer a sea-change,*
> *Into something rich and strange."*

George Gordon, Lord Byron

Byron was born in 1788 in London. While he was still a baby, his father ran away to France and died there within three years, leaving Byron to be raised by a mother who was violent towards him.

They went to live in Aberdeen as Catherine Byron was Scottish, and Byron first went to school there. After the death of his great-uncle Byron became a Lord at the age of ten, and they moved to Newstead Abbey, the family estate near Nottingham. After studying at Harrow, Byron went to Cambridge. It was during this time that he published his poems in a book called *Hours of Idleness*, which was poorly reviewed.

Coming of age, Byron took his place in the House of Lords, and then set off on a tour of Greece, Portugal, Spain and Turkey, beginning his great poem *Childe Harolde*. This was an immediate success and when he came back to London he found he was a celebrity overnight.

Byron was in debt, and unhappy with his roving life. He tried to settle down in marriage, but this was a failure, and after his wife of just one year, Annabella Milbanke, had borne him a child, she left him. This caused him great unpopularity and public opinion turned against him.

Because of this, he left England in 1816 for the last time, and travelled to Italy, where he became close to Shelley. He continued writing such great poems as *Don Juan,* and when, in 1823, his love of freedom drew him to Greece, he joined the struggle there as the Greeks fought to be free from Turkey. Although he became a hero, and did much to help the Greeks, he didn't live to see the success of his cause. He died after catching a fever, and his body was taken back to Britain. He was buried at Hucknall Torkard, in Nottinghamshire, in 1824.

WORDS, WORDS, WORDS!

You might just be surprised where our everyday words came from, once upon a time. Here are a few words with interesting histories – all you have to do is work out whether the origins below are actually true, or false!

Hawker:

nowadays, this means anyone who goes from place to place selling goods, or has a market stall. But once 'hawker' was a word belonging to the ancient art of falconry and meant a foot-traveller going around from castle to castle, selling trained falcons and spaniels to the noblemen who practised falconry. So the meaning hasn't changed too much through the years!

Stetson:

everyone must be familiar with this word, evoking the Wild West and its wilder cowboys. And even today many Westerners wouldn't be seen dead without their Stetsons! The story behind the word belongs to John B. Stetson, the son of a Philadelphia hatter, who went West to try a cure for his tuberculosis. While there he made a wide-brimmed hat from rabbit skin, which attracted a lot of attention from the ranchers and cowboys. Orders for the hat poured in, and John B. Stetson made his fortune.

Mews:

we associate stables and coach-houses with the word 'Mews' – often very rich land-owners will own several mews. The Royal Mews stood where the National Gallery is today and they were built for James I and VI on the site of a much older falcons' outhouse. 'Mews' is still another descendant from the age of falconry. The Latin verb is *mutare*, to change, and while the falcons were kept in this outhouse they went through a 'moulting' process, or mewing. These days, any building or house which was connected with stables at any time can be called 'The Mews' – the link with birds is well forgotten!

Haggard:

is another old falconry term, and it described a fierce, untamed falcon which was kept in captivity by the falconers but not trained. It would be over a year old. The word came to mean fierce and wild, as it changed to describe other things apart from birds. And from there it's just a short distance to the rather unflattering word we know now!

Big-Wig:

this is slang, meaning someone important – or just pompous. But in the eighteenth century calling someone a 'big-wig' was meant to be taken quite seriously. In those days, everyone wore wigs, even the gentlemen of the time – and schoolboys wore wigs and cocked hats! In fact, your trade or profession could be distinguished by your wig, and the more important and powerful you were, the bigger your wig – hence the expression.

Fed-up

do you ever feel 'fed-up'? Falcons used to – yes, it's another word we've taken from that sport. You see, falconry was called 'the sport of kings' and some of its expressions are nearly a thousand years old! Of course falconry still goes on today, but it's no longer such an all-important occupation as it once was. But to go back to being 'fed-up', this was what a tercel, or male hawk which had been given a good meal, would be called, as after eating well the bird wouldn't feel very much like flying from the wrist to kill, and sport would be useless. Through the years we have come to use the expression when feeling sluggish or bored – there's not much difference there from what the falcon probably felt!

Have you decided which stories were true and which false? Well, they were all true!

LANDMARKS AROUND THE WORLD

STATUE OF LIBERTY

The Statue of Liberty stands, towering 305 feet high over Liberty Island, off the channel of New York harbour. France gave the statue to the United States in 1884 as a symbol of 'Liberty Enlightening the World'.

The project was initiated by Frédéric Bartholdi, a French sculptor, who later executed the work. Begun in 1847, the

SAN SALVADOR'S CATHEDRAL

San Salvador is the capital of El Salvador, the smallest country in the Western Hemisphere. A tropical republic, El Salvador lies along the Pacific Ocean on the west coast of Central America. It is a beautiful land of volcanoes, mountain lakes, and picturesque beaches.

RUINS OF MACHU PICCHU

Machu Picchu, situated about 50 miles north-west of Cusco, in Peru, is the site of what was once an ancient Inca city. The stone structures forming the ruins of Machu Picchu stand on a mountain over 6,000 feet high. The ruins were discovered in 1911 by the American explorer Hiram Bingham.

Inca Indians developed an empire in South America before the arrival of the Spaniards. The Inca were conquered by Spanish troops in the 1500s after years of fighting. Inca civilisation was at its peak between 1450 and 1532, the empire stretching for more than 2,500 miles from north to south. It had its centre in the Andes Mountains of present-day Peru.

San Salvador's Cathedral, Spanish Gothic in style, has a background of extinct volcanoes. It was built of wood to give it protection from the earthquakes that frequently strike the capital.

TAJ MAHAL

The Taj Mahal which stands at Agra in northern India, is actually a tomb, one of the most beautiful and costly tombs in the world. The Indian ruler Shah Jahan ordered it to be built in memory of his favourite wife, whose title *Mumtaz-i-Mahal,* meaning 'pride of the palace', gave the building its name.

The Taj Mahal is made from white marble and rests on an eight-sided platform of red sandstone. Each side is 130 feet long. The dome covering the central part of the building is 70 feet in diameter and 120 feet high. The Taj Mahal stands in a garden, where pools reflect the building. The bodies of Shah Jahan and his wife lie in a vault below.

enlarged and completed figure was assembled in pieces (copper on wood) on a framework designed by Gustave Eiffel, builder of the Eiffel Tower. The robed figure stands 151 feet high. On the base of the statue is a poem by Emma Lazarus, part of which reads:

Give me your tired, your poor,
Your huddled masses yearning to breathe free,
The wretched refuse of your teeming shore.
Send these, the homeless, tempest-tost, to me.
I lift my lamp beside the golden door.

THE LOUVRE

One of the world's finest museums, the Louvre in Paris is also the largest art museum and palace in the world, and covers almost 50 acres on the north bank of the River Seine. The Louvre contains the French Ministry of Finance and has seven departments holding collections of art treasures, including paintings, sculptures and examples of the decorative arts. There are numerous exhibits from ancient Egypt, Greece and Rome. The Louvre has about 5,000 paintings, covering almost every period of art, and these works may be seen in the museum's 140 exhibition rooms and eight miles of galleries. In the Grand Gallery, 900 feet long, may be seen Leonardo's famous *Mona Lisa*. Displayed on the first floor are masterpieces which include the sculptures *Venus de Milo* and the *Winged Victory of Samothrace*, an ancient Greek statue.

The first Louvre was built as a Gothic fort by King Philip Augustus, in the 1100s. The main portions of the palace were constructed during the reign of King Louis XIV.

THE PYRAMIDS

The huge structures known as Pyramids were used by ancient peoples as tombs and temples. The most famous Egyptian Pyramids are the three standing near Giza (or Gizeh), and these pyramids are among the oldest monuments built by man. The largest of them, the *Great Pyramid*, was one of the Seven Wonders of the ancient world. Built by the Pharaoh Khufu during the 2,600s B.C., it towers to a height of 450 feet, and the base covers about 13 acres. The second pyramid of the group, which is 447½ feet high, was built by Khafre, who ruled shortly after Khufu. The third, 204 feet high, was built by Menkaure, Khafre's successor. There are about 80 Egyptian pyramids still standing, most of them in groups on the west side of the River Nile. The pyramids were built as royal tombs.

TOWER OF LONDON

The Tower of London, which stands on the north bank of the River Thames in London, is a mediaeval castle and includes an ancient fortress, a prison, an early Norman chapel and a former royal residence. The group of buildings is surrounded by a high stone wall and a moat. The Tower today is a peaceful place, a showplace and museum frequented by eager tourists and sightseers. The Corps of Yeomen Warders, sometimes referred to as *Beefeaters*, help to guard the crown jewels, which are kept in the Wakefield Tower. In the museum is an extensive collection of armour, begun by Henry VIII. Soldiers from the regiments of foot-guards usually provide the Tower's garrison.

The Tower of London holds an important place in English history. The construction of the Tower was started by William the Conqueror and, until the reign of James I, the Tower was a royal residence. Many famous people, however, have been imprisoned there. Sometimes the prisoners were taken there by boat, entering by the river entrance known as *Traitor's Gate*. Among the famous prisoners to have been there are Lady Jane Grey, Anne Boleyn, Sir Walter Raleigh and Sir Thomas More. The last well-known prisoner there was William Joyce, sometimes called 'Lord Haw Haw'; Joyce was confined in the Tower until his execution for treason in 1946.

PANTHEON

The Pantheon, standing in the centre of Rome, is one of the finest and best-preserved examples of ancient Roman architecture.

It was built by the Romans as a temple in honour of their gods; its name actually means 'of all the gods'. The original Pantheon was built in Rome by Agrippa in 27 B.C. In 123 A.D. Hadrian built the great central space called the *rotunda*, subsequently altered in design by Septimius Severus and Caracalla. The rotunda, in the shape of a circle, now forms the main part of the building. At the top of the dome, in the centre, is a window about 30 feet in diameter, through which comes the only light entering the building. The magnificent *portico* (porch) belonged to Agrippa's original temple, and across the front of it stand sixteen great Corinthian columns.

A QUESTION OF COLOUR

WHERE IS, AND WHO LIVES IN THE WHITE HOUSE?

The White House is the official residence of the President of the United States of America. It is a freestone building, painted white, hence its name, and it stands in Washington, DC. The corner stone of the White House was laid by George Washington.

WHO OR WHAT IS BLUE JOHN?

Blue John, named after a miner named John Kirk who first discovered it in a mine which also bears the same name in Castleton in Derbyshire, is a blue fluorspar, a mineral of calcium fluoride also known as 'Derbyshire spar'.

WHERE WOULD YOU FIND A BLACK WIDOW?

In tropical America and the southern United States. The Black Widow is one of the most poisonous of all the spiders, the female having a deadly bite which is not always counteracted by a person being given anti-poison serum . . . so beware the Black Widow!

WHAT IS A 'CLOUDED YELLOW'?

The Clouded Yellow is a butterfly found in almost every county in Britain. Its name belies its colour as it is orange with black borders, and both sexes have a black spot near the centre of the forewings and a deep orange spot in the middle of the hind wings.

WHO WAS THE CAPTAIN OF THE GOLDEN HIND?

Sir Francis Drake, who was knighted on board the Golden Hind by Elizabeth I in April 1581. The ship had originally been called the Pelican but it was rechristened the Golden Hind in 1578 near the straits of Magellan.

WHAT IS A RED LETTER DAY?

Today we say a red letter day is a special day when something exciting happens, a day to remember. The phrase still recalls the days when calendars marked certain church days and saints' days in red to make them stand out from ordinary days, which were marked in black.

WHAT IS A GREY GURNARD?

The least colourful of a species of three very unusual European fishes. It has slate grey colouring with a little green and purple added here and there. The grey gurnard is also the smallest of the species, a fact which is rather unfortunate for these small fish as it makes them easy prey for bigger fish!

WHERE WOULD YOU FIND A GREEN ROOM?

In a theatre. It is the place where actors wait near the stage for their entrance or to rehearse their lines, and it is so called because long ago this room was painted green as a pleasant contrast to the harsh glare of the stage.

FIFTY FASCINATING FACTS

Utterly true but sometimes amazing information.

BEWARE OF THE BULL
A bull's front legs are shorter than its back ones, enabling it to run faster going uphill than down.

PAMPERED PUSSY
Rather than tempt fate, when a party of thirteen arrives at the Savoy Hotel, London, for dinner, an extra place is laid for the hotel cat.

YOU ONLY LIVE ONCE
There is enough explosive on earth to wipe out mankind 50,000 times.

GALLON OF INK, PLEASE
In pence to the mile, it is cheaper to run a motorbike than a ballpoint pen.

HELLO, XLZPTZ SPEAKING
There is enough telephone cable under New York to reach Venus.

CHEEKY MONKEY
An art student in Pretoria who submitted a chimpanzee's pictures instead of his own was awarded a pass mark by examiners.

DEEP FREEZE
A lizard discovered inside a block of ice buried 33ft below ground level in Siberia, was found to be alive.

GOING UP
The three astronauts who spent twelve weeks in space on the Skylab mission had grown two inches taller by the time they returned to Earth.

FISH AND CHIPS
In Las Vegas some casinos have floating gambling tables in the swimming pools.

BARE-FACED PIGGERY
At the turn of the century, a shaved bear dressed in female clothing was exhibited as 'The Pig-Woman', a fortune-teller whose grunted replies were prompted by a man beneath the table with a sharp stick.

SWEET TEETH
One third of the world's boiled sweets are eaten in Britain.

OLD SCHOOL TIES
Eighteen of the forty-six Prime Ministers to govern Britain went to Eton.

PASSING FANCY
Inmates who escaped from Sing Sing prison could rely on a change of clothes at the home of millionaire Whitelaw Reid, who kept two suits hanging in an outside barn for that purpose.

UNSTEADY AS SHE GOES
In 1590 the Royal Navy beer ration was one gallon per sailor per day. In 1731 sailors had the choice of half a pint of rum or a pint of wine.

ARMLESS DEPRESSION?
Squids in captivity often commit suicide by eating their own tentacles.

OPEN HOUSE
2,500 pints of beer are sold in the House of Commons bar in London every week.

GIVE GENEROUSLY
Duelling in Uruguay is legal only on one condition – that both parties are registered blood donors.

BEWARE OF THE BEAR
When Lord Byron was at Cambridge there was a rule forbidding students to keep dogs in their rooms. Byron kept a bear.

BIRTH PAINS
Although the kiwi and the hen are virtually the same size, the kiwi's egg is eight times bigger. Kiwis are the only birds to hunt by smell.

ZIP!
If all the zips on earth were laid end to end they would reach to the moon and back twice.

DOLLAR WISE

Anyone wise enough to invest one dollar at 4 per cent compound interest on the day Jesus was born would now be worth the equivalent of one hundred solid gold balls, each one a thousand times as big as the earth.

PEACE ON EARTH

Just under three quarters of the earth's population live without radio, television, newspapers or telephones.

PROGRESS

The life expectancy of Swedish men and women is 71.7 years and 75.5 years respectively, the highest of all civilised countries and virtually the same as that of Australian Aborigines.

COLOURFUL WORLD

Apart from humans, monkeys are the only mammals capable of distinguishing different colours.

READY FOR BED

The average double bed requires four miles of walking and 25 hours work per year.

LIGHT SNACK

Frank Reese, a prisoner in a Texas jail, was responsible for a huge turnover in lightbulbs. He had been eating them. Pressed for a demonstration by television reporters, Frank downed fourteen bulbs and the sheriff's sunglasses.

SILENT MAJORITY

There are thirty dead people for every one living on earth.

THERMOMETERS OBSOLETE?

If you count the number of times a cricket chirps in one minute, subtract forty, divide by four and add fifty, you'll find the temperature Fahrenheit.

SAY CHEESE

Spacemen visiting other planets would do well not to smile. The smile is the only gesture man does not share with other earth animals. To most mammals, baring the teeth is an act of aggression.

STOP EMIGRATION

More people emigrate from the United Kingdom than from any other country.

WEIGHTY MATTER

A scientist who weighed people immediately before and after death concluded that the human soul weighs 21g.

FROZEN FOOD

A giant hailstone that landed in Essen, Germany, had a carp frozen inside it.

FISH AND SHIPS

Fish kept on board ships get seasick.

EQUAL PAY

Minstrels at the court of King Henry V were paid 1 shilling per day, the same as the Royal surgeon.

ROARING EXPORTS

Lions from Windsor Safari Park in England have been exported to Africa.

STRICT UPBRINGING

Young men in Malagasy Indian tribes must pay their fathers for the right to grow taller than them. While their fathers are alive they cannot shave or eat animal rumps.

LARGER THAN LIFE

Western sets in old Hollywood movies were built smaller than in real life to make the cowboys look big.

VINTAGE STUFF

The word vinegar comes from the French vin aigre, meaning sour wine.

VAMPIRES TAKE NOTE

American doctors in Florida have noticed that when the moon is in its second quarter some patients bleed up to twice as much during operations.

NO GUARANTEE

A Nigerian witch doctor who shot dead a prospective customer while demonstrating a bullet proof charm was sentenced to death in 1972.

SUPER TANKERS
The rudder of a giant oil tanker could provide parking space for nearly fifty cars if laid on its side.

WINDY
Workers on Japanese building sites sometimes use kites to carry bricks up tall buildings.

NOT CATS AND DOGS
During a freak storm in France, thousands of small toads rained down on the startled population.

SPIDER DRESSING
High-class barbers in Roman times used to dress the cuts of their clients with spiders' webs soaked in vinegar.

SLOW RISERS
Some species of snail have been known to sleep continuously for four years.

THICK-SKINNED
Although toads are capable of surviving 10,000 mg. of fluoracetic acid, as little as 1 mg. will kill a dog.

EARLY START
Female children in the Tiwi Islands in the Pacific are engaged before they are born. They are married at birth to the adult of their parents' choice.

WET LOT
The average American uses sixty gallons of water every day.

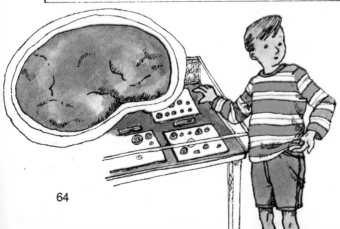

MUSEUM PIECE
A coin described as a 'Roman sesterce coin from between 135 and 138 A.D.' was removed from display when a nine-year-old boy recognised it as a plastic medallion given away with bottles of pop.

WHO KNOWS WHAT?
The average woman's brain weighs around 4 oz lighter than a man's. The brain of Neanderthal man was bigger than both.

WHY DO SOLDIERS WEAR KHAKI?

Soldiers wear khaki for camouflage, of course, to ensure that they blend with their background and make them less easily spotted by their enemies.

In early times camouflage was not so important to soldiers; fighting at that time was usually hand to hand, and distinctive uniforms were necessary so that the combatants could discriminate between friend and foe. The uniforms were as colourful as possible, and were covered with feathers, ribbons and other decorations to give the fighting men a sense of unity, a feeling of belonging to, and being a part of their own regiment.

But with the invention of the breech-loading gun and long-range artillery, camouflage became very important indeed, as the British soldiers fighting in the American War of Independence found to their cost. Many of the Americans had no uniform as such, and wore their usual hunting shirts, whose neutral colour gave them good protection. The British soldiers, in their red coats and white breeches, presented perfect targets, and were unable to melt into the landscape.

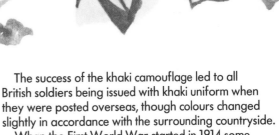

In the 1840s Lieutenant Harry Lumsden was forming a regiment of cavalry and infantry in northern India, and was given permission to arm and dress his men as he wished. Since their duties would involve skirmishes with the natives he decided that his men should wear uniforms the colour of the local ground, so that they would be inconspicuous, and had cloth specially dyed locally. It was called khaki after the Urdu word for dusty, and when Lumsden's regiment went into action in 1849 they were known as the 'Mudlarks'.

The success of the khaki camouflage led to all British soldiers being issued with khaki uniform when they were posted overseas, though colours changed slightly in accordance with the surrounding countryside.

When the First World War started in 1914 some cavalry regiments wore their traditional colourful uniforms, but they soon changed to khaki, the colour of the mud in the trenches and the dust of the roads they had to travel.

Today soldiers all over the world dress in khaki, glad of the protection it affords them. The bright, colourful uniforms that once glamourized war have disappeared.

IS IT TRUE?

Noah's Ark

The Book of Genesis in the Old Testament tells of a Great Flood which was God's way of punishing men for their wicked ways. This flood destroyed all life, with the exception of Noah, his family, and those animals he took with him on the Ark.

No one will ever know if Noah really existed, or if he really built an Ark, but what is known is that there *was* a great flood in the land known as Mesopotamia, between the rivers Tigris and Euphrates, completely submerging what was to the inhabitants the whole earth. There are three proofs of this flood, and the first lies in another story, the Epic of Gilgamesh.

This story was translated from a series of stone tablets found during the excavation of the royal library at Ninevah, the ancient capital of Mesopotamia. The story is 4,000 years old – older than the Bible – and tells of a great flood sent by the gods to destroy the human race. Gilgamesh was warned by one of the gods, so he built an ark and took his family and animals on board.

The second proof is the Ancient Sumerian king-list, compiled around 2,000 BC. This starts with the names of eight kings, then it states that 'the flood came', and after the flood 'a

kingship was sent down from the gods'.

The final piece of evidence was found in 1929, during Sir Leonard Woolley's excavations of the Royal Cemetery in the Euphrates valley. As he dug down, he discovered various layers of broken pottery, flints and the remains of buildings. Then he came to a layer of clean, water-laid mud, eight feet deep, and under that, more pots and flints. This suggested that there had been a flood with water at least twenty-five feet deep, and other excavations in the area drew the same conclusion.

The Man in the Iron Mask

In the famous novel by Alexander Dumas, the man in the iron mask is kept a miserable prisoner in the Bastille, and is portrayed as the twin brother of Louis XIV – or maybe even the king himself.

In fact, there was a masked prisoner in the Bastille during the reign of Louis XIV, but his mask was of velvet and he lived in style and comfort. He was guarded by two Musketeers at all times, and they had orders to kill him if he unmasked. He was arrested in 1669, and spent the rest of his life a prisoner, dying thirty-four years later. He was forbidden under pain of death to speak of anything but his everyday needs, and his name was never revealed – he was buried under a false name. Who was he?

No one will ever know for certain, but the most likely theory is that the prisoner was the true father of Louis XIV. Louis XIII and his queen had been childless for thirteen of their twenty-two years of marriage, and had lived apart for years until Cardinal Richelieu brought about a brief reconciliation. Shortly after this the queen gave birth to a son, and it is probable that the father was not Louis but some nobleman, chosen to make certain that there was a royal heir. Certainly the young Louis looked nothing like his father.

The theory goes that the real father was sent abroad to avoid any scandal, and when he returned, perhaps hoping for favours from his son who was now the all-powerful 'Sun King', he was arrested and hidden away. He probably looked too much like the king for comfort. Louis couldn't bring himself to murder his own father, so he had him gaoled for life instead.

But of course, no one will ever know for sure who the mysterious masked man was, for his secret was buried with him.

WHO INVENTED . . .

. . . THE MATCH?

From earliest times, in all parts of the world, people have made fire by rubbing a hard stick against a soft stick so that soft flakes of wood, sloughed off by the hard stick, started to smoulder. Another way was to use flint, a very hard stone, striking it against a lump of iron to produce sparks.

Until the eighteenth century, the only improvement on these primitive methods was the tinder box, which contained a piece of steel, flint and some dry tinder for the sparks to ignite. Tinder was often pieces of charred linen or silk; sometimes even dried fungus. The process of raising a spark could be very time-consuming, especially if the tinder was cold and damp.

Matches were first invented as a method of transferring the flame from the smouldering tinder to where it was needed. Splinters of pine were used, their ends dipped in sulphur, which flared easily and made dangerous fumes. It is thought that the Chinese used similar sulphur matches as long ago as the sixth century. For a time sulphur matches were cheap and popular, but still the tinder box was needed to make the initial spark. All over Europe scientists were trying to do away with the need for the tinder box.

The first real breakthrough came in 1827 when English chemist John Walker invented a match with *all* the fire-producing compounds in its head. He called them 'friction lights', because the flame was created by friction, and soon the idea was taken up by large manufacturers who made them in their millions.

However, with friction lights there was a danger that they would ignite accidentally. A Swedish scientist came up with the idea of the safety match in 1845, putting only some of the chemicals on the match head and the rest on the side of the box. The match would only ignite when struck against the box.

...THE CIGARETTE?

The cigarette was the last method of taking tobacco to be developed. Previously it had been smoked in pipes and cigars, inhaled as snuff (in powder form) and chewed. Tobacco itself was brought to Europe and the rest of the world when Columbus discovered America, and it was thought to have marvellous medicinal properties.

No one could be said to have actually invented the cigarette. It began as a kind of cigar. Cigars were made in Spain, by hand, and were very expensive. The story goes that the beggars of the Spanish city Seville used to collect up the cigar butts thrown into the street, shred the tobacco from them and roll it into paper, which they smoked. They called these concoctions *cigarillos*: 'poor man's smokes'.

Whether or not this is true, the idea of smoking tobacco rolled in a piece of paper spread slowly through eighteenth century Europe until it reached France. Here the new smokes were given the name 'cigarettes'. There were several reasons for their popularity; they were cheaper than cigars, less trouble than a pipe, and more fashionable than snuff. A man would carry his own tobacco and a booklet of paper from which he would form his own cigarettes.

Cigarette smoking finally reached Britain in the 1850 when soldiers fighting in the Crimean War picked up the habit from the Turks and Russians. From there it spread to America, where tobacco had first been discovered, centuries before.

At first, cigarettes were made by hand, but in 1880 an American invented a machine to do the job, increasing the numbers made every year from 500 million to 4,000 million – in America alone! Today, a cigarette machine can make 12,000 to 16,000 cigarettes every minute.

THE PLANTAGENET REIGN

Who were the Plantagenets?

They were a family who ruled Britain from 1154 to 1485. Famous Plantagenet kings include Richard I, John, Edward I and Richard II. In 1485 Richard III died fighting against Henry Tudor, and so the Plantagenet dynasty died, after more than three hundred years of power.

The first Plantagenet was Count Geoffrey of Anjou, who was the father of Henry II. He was given the name Plantagenet because of the sprig of broom he always wore (Plantagenet is taken from the latin for sprig, *planta*, and *genista* for broom plant). Henry II was an ambitious king, and became very powerful indeed, possessing immense areas of France and adding Ireland to his list of conquests. In later years, however, he had trouble with the Church, and ended up causing the assassination of Thomas à Becket, Archbishop of Canterbury, while he was praying in the Cathedral. Thomas was declared a saint in 1172 and Canterbury became a shrine for many pilgrimages there. Despite this tragedy, Henry went on to strengthen his reign and introduce many reforms, such as creating the jury system.

For many years there was a feud between two Plantagenet brothers. One, Richard the Lionheart, was king in England while fighting the Crusades abroad. Strong and courageous as his nickname showed, he was cast as the hero in the battle between himself and John, who became king after Richard's death in the Third Crusade. John's nickname was 'Lackland', as his father had left him no estates. He turned out to be a weak king, forced to sign the foundation of democratic liberty, the Mgna Carta, in 1215, allowing the clergy and nobles to take an active part in government.

Little more than a century later, one of the greatest Plantagenet kings came to power. Edward I helped to create the English Parliament, and allowed the 'burgess' class – representatives of the people rather than nobles – to have their say. He also conquered Wales, whose lands were owned by Celtic tribes. Later he gave the Welsh his new-born son as the 'Prince of Wales'. Ever since that, the eldest sons of all the sovereigns of England have held this title.

Edward also tried to conquer Scotland. He occupied the country in 1296 and managed to put down every revolt there for ten years,

JOHN

EDWARD I

HENRY II

RICHARD I

EDWARD III

HENRY V

HENRY VI

EDWARD IV

RICHARD III

executing heroes such as William Wallace. But he never managed to control Scotland during his reign, and for many more years Scotland managed to hold on to her independence, helped by France, her old ally, against the English.

There was no love lost between the English and the French, and in 1337, in the reign of Edward III, the Hundred Years' War began. The pretext for the war was the contested succession to the throne of France: Edward claimed he should be the next French king. But underlying this was the bitterness caused by the French aiding the Scottish.

The first period of war ended victoriously for Edward when he defeated the French at Crecy and Poitiers, gaining large amounts of French territory in the process. Later, however, the war went badly with him, casting a shadow on the last years of his reign.

This long war reached its climax in Henry V's reign, when he routed the French at Agincourt and forced the French to recognise him as successor to the throne. By a twist of fate, however, Henry died and the race between the English and the French began to Reims Cathedral, where the kings of France were crowned. The English had with them the baby Henry VI, while the French, led by Joan of Arc, had Charles VI's son, the 'dauphin'. Joan of Arc defeated the English and managed to have the French child crowned Charles VII.

Less than a few years after the end of this great and bloody war, another war raged under Plantagenet rule – the Wars of the Roses. This was a civil war between the houses of York and Lancaster, and the issue at stake was the throne of England. The existing king, Henry VI, who was to have been crowned at Reims Cathedral, had grown up to be a half-wit. His cousin, Edward the Duke of York, deposed him and had himself crowned king as Edward IV. Supporters of Henry VI took up arms against him, and the war ended only in 1481 on the death of Edward.

Edward's two sons, one of whom would have succeeded him, were both killed by Edward's brother

Richard, ruthlessly determined to be king himself. In fact he did become Richard III, but hatred rose up against him and the son-in-law of Edward, Henry Tudor, defeated Richard in the battle of Bosworth and became Henry VII, the first Tudor king. This year, 1485, saw the end of the Plantagenet reign.

THE INDIANS OF NORTH AMERICA

IROQUOIS

TEPEE

SIOUX

PUEBLO

The North American Indians lived in the USA for thousands of years before Columbus. From the border with Canada to the swamps of what is now Florida countless tribes existed, each with their own languages, cultures and ways of life. Some were hunters, some fishermen, some simply seed-gatherers in the arid deserts of the west. They were peaceful, like the Seminole, or Cree; warlike, like the Sioux. 'Sioux' means 'enemy' in an Indian language (they called themselves the Dakota) but this fierce tribe were feared by many other American Indians.

Different climates meant Indians built different homes. The Navaho had earth-covered log shelters called hogans. The Pueblo built their 'blocks of flats' with adobe, sun-dried brick. The nomad tribes lived in tepees and wickiups, which could be moved easily from place to place.

They lived on maize, beans, pemmican (dried meat and grease), peppers, tomatoes and ground nuts. They were the first race to gather rubber and grow tobacco! They also hunted buffalo and bison.

The American Indians loved trading, and would follow long trails to barter goods and precious metals for wampum, a kind of shell money. The chief of the tribe held power but there was also a council of all men in the tribe. Before the coming of the white man war was thought of almost as a ceremonial game, a test of bravery, but the battles the Indians fought later were for their lands and survival.

TOTEM POLE

NAVAHO LOOM

SIOUX CHILD

SHAMAN

The North American Indians had their heroes, too – men like Cochise, the Apache chief who fought against the United States for eleven years before making peace, and Crazy Horse and Sitting Bull, who both played decisive parts in the victory of the Battle of the Little Big Horn in 1876, when the Sioux wiped out the American forces of General Custer.

There were over a million Indians in America when the mass of Europeans settled. These people wanted the Indian lands and pushed the retreating tribes further and further west, while the government made treaty after treaty with the Indians. As each treaty failed there were small but savage wars between the Indians and the new 'Americans'. Three factors caused, in part, the downfall of the traditional Indian way of life: the fact that the settlers had guns and also horses, both of which were unknown to the tribes, and lastly the influx of alcohol, 'firewater' as the Indians called it, which had a disastrous effect on the Indian way of life. All these pressures, and more, meant that tribal traditions and standards were broken down and by the nineteenth century many Indians were being settled in reservations, where their children grew up, rootless and confused about their racial identity.

Religion was very important, and many different gods were worshipped. There was a totem in each tribe, embodying the spirit of their clan. The shaman or medicine man, a kind of religious doctor, cured sicknesses and wounds with herbal remedies such as quinine, which is used in the modern world. There was a belief that a life existed after death, and that they would go to the 'happy hunting ground'.

Indians were skilled at embroidery – they made clothes from cloth and sewed animal skins together cleverly to make coverings, tepees and saddles – weaving, making baskets, jewellery, beadwork and pottery.

Music was important and they made many kinds of instruments: castanets, drums, rattles, flutes and pipes, made from bone and cane. Although they did not write as we do, they drew picture figures and often kept records of years on animal hides. Their languages were intricate and diverse – often different tribes had to use sign-language as they couldn't understand each other.

IS ART YOUR SUBJECT?

1
Who painted the ceiling of the Sistine Chapel in Rome?

2
Who painted *The Artist in His Studio*?

3
Which artist specialised in drawings and paintings of Tudor aristocrats, including some fine studies of Henry VIII?

4
Who painted the very famous landscape, *The Hay-Wain*?

5
This Dutch painter was famous for his use of light and shade, and among his best paintings are *The Night Watch* and *The Anatomy Lesson of Professor Tulp*. Who was he?

6
Which French artist made informal pastel studies of ballet dancers, as in *The Dancing Class*?

7
The Laughing Cavalier must be one of the most famous paintings in the world. Who painted it?

8
This American artist is one of the most well-known of the 'action painters', and he uses a drip technique to produce his paintings. Who is he?

Check your answers on page 191

IT'S ALL TRUE!

There were only one hundred television sets in the United Kingdom in November 1936 when the first public television broadcast went on the air. Now there are estimated to be 96 sets to every 100 people in some parts of the world.

The shark has the most remarkable digestive powers. In its stomach is a vitriol-like fluid, enabling the fish to digest almost any substance. The iron on a horse's hoof swallowed by a shark had, when the shark was caught and cut open, begun to disintegrate. This fluid, spilled on a man's bare flesh, will remove the skin as if the flesh had been scorched with fire.

Most typists are able to type from 30 – 60 words per minute under test conditions, but an American typist has been recorded typing 170 words in one minute. The *slowest* typists are the Chinese because their written language, and hence their typewriter, is so complicated that even the most skilled operator cannot type more than 11 words in one minute.

Do you have trouble with maths at school? You are not alone. The Temiar peoples of Malaysia in the Indian Ocean have no understanding of any number greater than three! When a number higher than three is mentioned their faces show complete bewilderment.

The word 'boudoir' comes from the French *bouder*, meaning 'to sulk'. In eighteeth-century England, men as well as women had these sulking rooms.

75

WHAT WOULD WE DO WITHOUT IT?

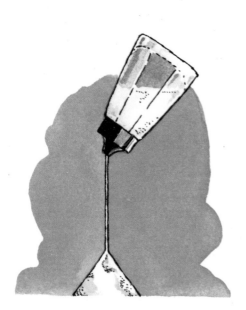

SALT

Everyone needs salt to stay alive: it's absolutely essential to our systems, and is found in most of the foods we eat. Britain alone produces two and a half million tons every year – and every ounce is used up!

In fact, we need salt so much that when a group of criminals in Sweden were once given the choice to do without salt for a month, as an alternative to capital punishment, those who agreed were dead within the month! We take salt very much for granted these days, but in earlier times it was very highly prized; wars were fought simply to obtain salt, and it is true that as late as this century the people of Sierre Leone were willing to sell their families for salt.

There is a fascinating city made of salt, carved underground in the salt mines of Wieliczka, Poland. You can walk around admiring churches, monuments, streets and even railway stations – all carved from salt! And to prove just how important salt used to be to us, our word 'salary' comes from the Latin 'salarium', meaning money for salt.

COAL

Coal is something which we all need in some way or other. We need coal to produce heat and light for our homes and offices; our industry needs coal to provide many commercial and household goods to export all over the world.

Different types of coal are often found in a coalfield. There are 'coking coals', for instance which, when mined, aren't used for home consumption but are valuable for the blast furnaces of a steel works. Then there is anthracite, a hard kind of coal which burns with a very intense heat.

Coal is still mined today by men going down into the earth and risking their lives to bring the coal from the seams up to the surface. Despite a great many new safety measures mining is still a difficult and dangerous job. At least the practice of taking children to work down the mineshafts has ceased now, although pit-ponies are still used to pull loads of coal underground.

There are quite a few mines in Britain, mostly in Wales, Scotland and North-East England. A world famous mining area is that of the Ruhr valley in Western Germany.

WOOL

Wool has kept us warm since very ancient times when man first domesticated sheep, and even in this age of synthetic fibres wool still remains a firm favourite with most of us. Britain, especially, has a lot of sheep grazing on the hills of Scotland, Wales and Ireland, and has a thriving wool industry.

Britain was very important when it came to wool-producing in the Middle Ages, and a sack of wool became a status symbol of wealth, hence the Lord Chancellor's seat in the House of Lords becoming known as the Woolsack. All in all, the sheep population of the world is about 970,000,000!

When shorn, the sheep's fleece is matted and oily and unfit for spinning, so the fleece must be washed and 'carded' before going on to the next process. Once spun, the wool goes on to be woven into the woollen clothes and rugs, carpets, etc., we are familiar with in the shops. In the Middle Ages the Flemish were celebrated weavers; these days Bradford and Leeds are well-known for their fine weaving!

SOAP

This is something that everyone uses at least once every day! But about a hundred years ago soap was so expensive that only very rich people could afford it.

Soap is made from different fats and oils. We import these oils from other countries, as we need coconut and olive oils and whale fats, as well as some other animal fats. These oils and fats are all heated up together, with caustic soda, which is an alkaline solution. Heating these ingredients produces glycerine, which is used for other purposes, so this is separated from the soap mixture.

The soap, which by now has formed a curd, is boiled again, to remove all traces of salt. After this, it is given its perfume and colourings. Left to cool in long bars, it's then cut up and wrapped for us to buy.

Soap is really a 'dirt loosener'. It dissolves in water, so the soap in in the water surrounds the specks of dirt on our hands, and loosens them from the skin. Then, as we move our hands in the water, the specks float away with the water, leaving our hands clean and fresh!

OTHER TIMES – OTHER FASHIONS

Fashions are changing all the time, and what you wear today might send a Victorian into fits of giggles! Just how much do you know about the way people dressed in the past? Many of their everyday accessories and styles would be completely unknown to us . . . but some others might be more familiar!

The ruff was a wide white collar which originated in Spain in the sixteenth century when it was worn by everyone – men, women and children! It became high fashion in 1575 and grew so much that by 1586 it became known as a cartwheel! Called *Duttenkragen* in Germany, the ruff was made of fine linen, stitched, folded, starched and stayed with wire to keep it close to the neck. Germans wore it until the eighteenth century and for a long time it was considered a traditional part of the Jewish dress.

Gaiters were a covering of cloth or leather for the ankle and lower leg, and they made their first appearance in France during the seventeenth century, with typical side-fastenings. They don't have soles, they cover the shoe and the lower leg, protecting them from rain and wet pavements. During the eighteenth century they were mostly used with Army uniforms, and in the next century, with the advent of goloshes, gaiters lost their appeal.

The crinoline was a very famous fashion for quite a while; it was invented in Paris in 1840. This skirt was called after the material supporting it from underneath – and this skirt needed support, because it was massive! 'Crin' was the horse hair in the material, and 'linum' was the thread used to sew the underskirt. The crinoline itself was usually made of much more sumptuous material, such as satin or silk. Although the crinoline itself needed vast amounts of fabric, the fashion was to embellish it with extra flounces, and in 1859 the Empress Eugenie wore a crinoline with 103 such flounces! To produce such a wide, flowing effect the crinoline needed hoops to support the almost circular line, and one German factory made so many crinolines, with 60 yards of wire hoops in each, that the wire used would have been sufficient to span the globe at the equator thirteen times! The crinoline began to fade from fashion about 1870; it had many enemies who protested that the skirt was ugly, took up too much space and was cruel to the figure.

Lorgnettes were used up until the last century – perhaps your grandparents have seen them! They were spectacles on a long, elegant handle, and they weren't worn – just held up to the eyes by the handle. The upper classes found them popular during the eighteenth century, and it was generally women who used them. In the nineteenth century, using a lorgnette became a highly complicated and involved social game – rather as fans were used by younger women.

Toga, the Roman outer garment, was quite small to begin with, but later began to grow larger and more voluminous. The toga was usually semi-circular or elliptical in shape, and would measure about twelve feet wide and eighteen feet long! At night the toga would be draped around a dummy, in order that the carefully-placed folds should not crumple; but in time this kind of toga proved to be impractical for day to day use, and others were favoured. The *toga virilis* could be worn by all men, provided they were freemen and not slaves; the *toga praetexta* was worn by higher officials, and only consuls could wear the *toga palmata*. It was forbidden for slaves to wear togas.

Doublet was another word for the padded coat men wore underneath the breastplate of armour. During the fifteenth century the doublet became more important, being the main garment worn underneath the top coat or cloak. It would always have sleeves, and during its time it followed fashion closely, changing style many times. Sometimes it was slashed and puffed, sometimes tight-fitting. It grew shorter and shorter through the years, until in the seventeenth century it was replaced by the waistcoat which men wear today.

Galligaskins sound much more exciting than they really were! In fact, they were stockings for men, worn in the sixteenth century and during the first half of the seventeenth. They only reached the knees, and could be either padded or smooth round the hips. I wonder where their names came from? Knickerbockers, or Plus Fours, were reminiscent of galligaskins, but they were sports trousers, ending at the knee, worn in the Twenties and Thirties.

Would you have worn any of these strange-sounding things? Yes, you would – if you'd been born at the right time. And you would have thought that jeans and plimsolls looked very funny indeed – wouldn't you?

WAY OUT WEST

Which American President was born in a log cabin in Kentucky?

Abraham Lincoln. Later the family moved to Indiana where the family built a 'half-face' which was a three-sided shelter, framed with poles and thatched with bark. He ate wild berries and learned to shoot wild turkeys for food. Later still the family went by covered waggon to New Salem, and years later his new home became the White House in Washington, D.C.

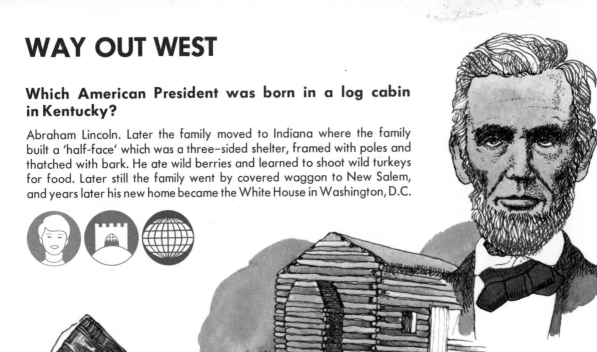

With what do you associate Jim Bowie?

The Bowie knife, which Bowie first used in a fight in Mississippi and which proved so effective that it was manufactured as a weapon, marketed as the Bowie knife. It was fashioned from a rasp used by blacksmiths and had a curved edge ending in a point. Jim Bowie was one of the gallant band who defended the Alamo in 1836.

How did the city of Wichita in Kansas get its name?

It was named after a tribe of Indians whose name means 'The men'. A living monument to these days of the old west still survives in the city today, recalling the origin of its name, in a section called 'Cowtown'. Cowtown contains the city's first jail, its first hotel and several early buildings. Today Wichita is also well known for the production of wheat, corn, pigs and poultry, and it also manufactures excellent farm implements.

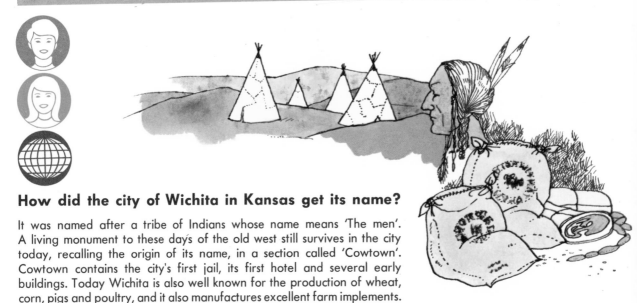

HOW IT WORKS
Electronic Calculator

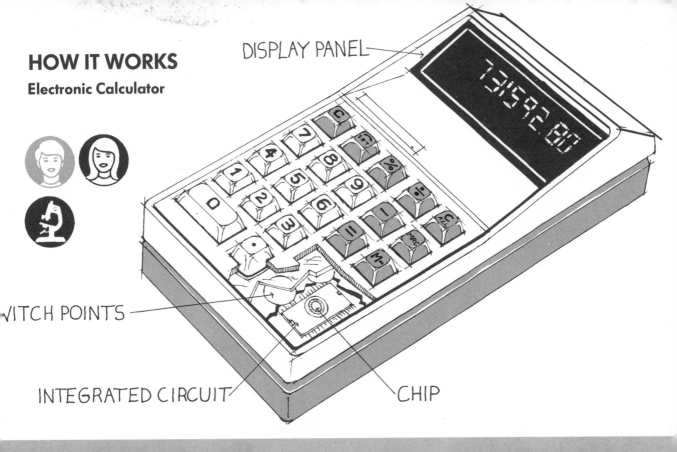

DISPLAY PANEL

SWITCH POINTS

INTEGRATED CIRCUIT

CHIP

The operations of an electronic calculator are not only very quick, they are also very basic. Most of the calculations are done using simple addition and subtraction, and a number system which has only two numbers, 0 and 1.

This *binary* (two-state) number system is used in calculators and other electronic devices, because they operate on a system of electronic switches, which at any time can only be in one of two states: off or on. In the binary code, 'off' is represented by 0, and 'on' by 1.

The calculator keyboard uses our usual (decimal) numbers, from 0 up to 9, on its keys, but when a key is pushed down, the calculator understands this in the binary equivalent, which is fed through a

'switch point', situated under the key, and from there into the heart of the calculator – the 'chip'.

This is a tiny integrated circuit, an incredible network of electronic components in a piece of silicon, itself smaller than a postage stamp.

The chip carries out the binary operations at the speed of light, and its answers are sent back to the display. The calculator converts binary into decimal again, using a 'decoder' (a circuit based on switches), and these decimals appear on the display panel, using LED, or light emitting diode, segments.

The space for each unit on the display has seven such segments, plus a decimal point, and each LED gives off a reddish glow when required. Different combinations of these segments light up any decimal

number from 0 up to 9, as the chip instructs through the switching circuit.

The chip adds in the standard binary way: $0 + 1 = 1$; $0 + 0 = 0$; and $1 + 1 = 10$ (equivalent of 2). And it subtracts by reversing this procedure.

The operations of multiplication and division are carried out by continued addition and subtraction, respectively. For example, to multiply 43 by 17, the calculator adds 43 seventeen times. This may seem slow to us, but electronically the answer is arrived at almost immediately.

Just try dividing 1,089 by 33, and see how long you take! How would the calculator solve this one? And because it works electronically, it can do harder sums in about the same amount of time. It would divide 582.31 by 34.9 as soon as add two and two!

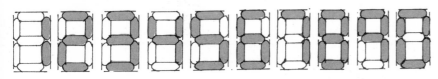

Seven LED segments that form any numeral: here are the combinations for each number, from 0 up to 9.

BRIDGES AND BRIDGE BUILDERS

The Forth Bridge was opened in 1890 and was for many years the longest bridge in Europe with a span of 1,700 feet.

The Lower Zambesi Bridge, built for the Central African railway, is over 2 miles long and has 33 main spans.

The Great Salt Lake Viaduct, made of timber, steel, brick and reinforced concrete, is 62,605 feet long in Utah, U.S.A.

Isambard Kingdom Brunel (1806-1889) was a famous bridge and railway engineer who was born in Portsmouth, although he went to Paris to study in 1820, when he was fourteen. He was later to build the Clifton Suspension bridge over the River Avon, in 1864, and the Tamar bridge in Cornwall in 1859. In 1883 he was appointed engineer to Great Western Railways.

Alexandre Gustave Eiffel was another talented bridge-designer who built bridges all over Europe. He is regarded as the father of iron and steel construction in France; his work is still admired today for its skill and versatility. His bridges can be seen in Portugal and in France where the Railway Viaduct over the River Truyere crosses a 406-foot deep ravine in a single span of 540 feet. This was for many years the highest bridge in the world. Because of his skill he was later to be commissioned to design the Eiffel Tower for the Paris Exposition of 1889.

In 1856 the Englishman Henry Bessemer developed a revolutionary process of producing steel cheaply from molten pig-iron inside a furnace or 'converter'. This proved to be a breakthrough in the construction of bridges.

EIFFEL TOWER

BRUNEL

FORTH BRIDGE

THE HISTORY OF HANDWRITING

The way we write is very important these days. Every child is taught how to form words on paper and we base a great deal of our everyday communication on handwriting. Apart from the ordinary handwriting which we all learn, some people are expert at the craft of beautiful writing called *calligraphy*.

The English alphabet developed from the alphabet that the Romans, in turn, adapted from the Greeks. Other alphabets, such as Russian and Chinese, use different letters with different shapes. These come from other sources.

Long ago, very few people could write. There were special employees, called *scribes*, who knew how to write, and they wrote letters and messages for their masters, who were rich and powerful men.

The scribes had to write very fast indeed, in order to include everything their masters dictated. Eventually this meant that the angular, separate letters of the Roman alphabet became more curved, much like our letters of the alphabet today. The Roman scribes also developed quill pens and parchment to write on.

Later it was the Christian monks who learned to write. They worked on the wonderful books of the Gospels, writing all the text by hand and painting the illustrations. They wrote in what was called the *Gothic* or *black letter* script.

As years passed the letters that were formed changed and became more fluid and compressed. Italian scribes at the Papal Chancery in Rome developed a graceful, oval, sloping way of writing which was known as Italic. This is popular today.

A more recent method of handwriting is called Copperplate. When handwriting manuals were being engraved on copper plates the engraver wrote with swirling, complex curves to show the perfection of his skill. Copperplate, although it needed special pens, was very popular in the nineteenth century.

GRATIAS AC IMMENSE TUE DOMIN PATER OM

deus que me indignum famulum ac miserum peccatorum nullis exhibentibus sed tuis n

Approve not of him who commend

Envy is always waiting where

WOMEN WHO WROTE

George Sand

George Sand, in fact, was a woman, born Amandine Dupin, Baronne Dudevant. She was a gifted writer and also a woman ahead of her time, who flouted the conventions of her age and shocked many people by her lifestyle.

After an unhappy marriage she fled to Paris and obtained a divorce, changing her name to George Sand and supporting herself and her two children with her writing. Her novels dealt with the issue of women's rights, and she was a tireless crusader for this cause, often demonstrating her own independence by wearing trousers – unheard of in the nineteenth century!

Her best-known novels are *The Haunted Pool,* written in 1846, and *The Master Bell Ringers,* written in 1853. She also had a long-lasting friendship with the famous composer Frederick Chopin. She died in 1876.

Louisa May Alcott

She was born in Pennsylvania in 1832 and began her working life as a servant, to eke out her family's income. She also became a skilled seamstress before turning to writing and making her fortune.

During the American Civil War Louisa May Alcott left home to be a nurse, and her letters to the family while she was away were later published. She began to see her poems and stories appear regularly in *The Atlantic Monthly,* and went on to be made editor of *Merry's Museum,* a children's magazine.

The novel she is most remembered for, *Little Women,* appeared a few years later, in 1868, and was loved at once by children and adults alike. One of the characters, the tomboy of the March family, Jo, was modelled largely on Louisa May Alcott herself. The book was so popular that she wrote two sequels, *Little Men* and *Jo's Boys.* Although Louisa May Alcott wrote about Jo's marriage in these books, she herself never married. She died in 1888.

Gertrude Stein

Gertrude Stein was born in 1874 in Pittsburgh. She attended Radcliffe College for Women, and later trained in medicine, but she gave her career up to travel through Europe and settle in Paris. There she began writing, and also befriending many struggling artists and poets who would one day be famous, like herself.

The nineteen twenties were Gertrude Stein's high point. She became the head of a cultural group which included F. Scott Fitzgerald, Ernest Hemingway and Sherwood Anderson. She called them 'the lost generation'. She was also friendly with Picasso and Matisse.

Her novels were unconventional, discarding grammar and punctuation in order to clarify her thoughts and ideas. *Three Lives,* written in 1909, is perhaps her best-known novel. She died in 1946.

Virginia Woolf

Virginia Woolf was a very original and perceptive writer, who was one of the first female exponents of the 'stream of consciousness' style of writing. Her novels are both impressionistic and finely-drawn. Born into a reputable English family, Virginia Woolf married Leonard Woolf, a critic, in 1912. Together they started the Hogarth Press, and their home became a meeting-place for critics, writers and artists. This group became known as 'the Bloomsbury Group', and published a fair deal of material.

Her own novels include *The Voyage Out,* written in 1915, and *The Lighthouse,* in 1927. Virginia Woolf drowned herself in 1941.

THE MONTHS OF THE YEAR

January was dedicated by the Romans to **Janus,** a two-faced god, who could look back on the old year, and forward to the new. It was, however, originally the eleventh month of the year.

Battle of Spion Kop, 1900

Captain Cook killed, 1779

February was originally the Roman month of purification prior to the new year, from the Latin *februo*, 'I purify by sacrifice'.

Slave trade abolished in British Empire, 1807

March was named after Mars, the Roman god of war. In the ancient Roman calendar it was the first month of the new year.

Gas first used in World War I, 1915 (Battle of Ypres)

April derives from the Latin *aperire*, to open, referring to the month when buds and blossoms open.

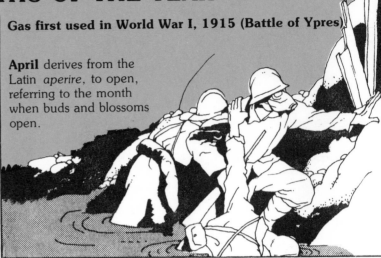

May was probably named after Maia, the Roman goddess of growth or increase, mother of Mercury. Alternatively its origin lies in the Latin word *majores*, meaning elders.

Joan of Arc burnt at the stake, 1431

June comes from either Juno, the Queen of Heaven, or from Junius, a clan name based on the Latin word *juvenis*, meaning young.

King John signed Magna Carta, 1215

Man lands on the Moon, 1969

July was named after Julius Caesar, by Mark Antony in 44 B.C.; this month was originally called *Quintilis*, or fifth month. Until the end of the eighteenth century July was pronounced to rhyme with truly.

August was changed from Sextilis to Augustus in 8 B.C., in honour of the first emperor, because it was his lucky month.

ROYAL MAIL ROYAL MAIL

Great Train Robbery, 1963

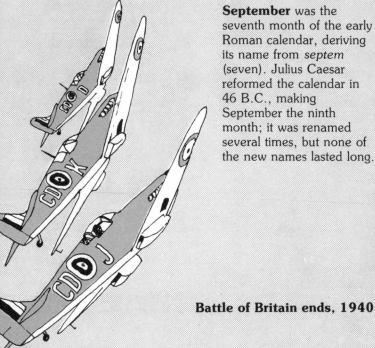

September was the seventh month of the early Roman calendar, deriving its name from *septem* (seven). Julius Caesar reformed the calendar in 46 B.C., making September the ninth month; it was renamed several times, but none of the new names lasted long.

Battle of Britain ends, 1940

October was originally the eighth Roman month, from *octo* (eight) and was held sacred to Mars.

Columbus reaches America, 1492

The Gunpowder Plot, 1605

November comes from *novem* (nine). Having changed July and August to commemorate great Romans, the Senate offered to rename November after Tiberius Caesar, but he declined.

Tay Bridge destroyed, 1879

December was originally the tenth month, from *decem* (ten).

HOW DID INN SIGNS ORIGINATE?

From earliest times it was important that traders and shopkeepers identified themselves to their customers. People could not read or write, and houses and shops were not numbered, so shopkeepers used to put up simple signboards outside their premises to let everyone know just what they had to offer.

When were signboards first used?

Tradesmen's signs existed in Greek and Roman times, and by the 17th century in England signs (and signwriting) flourished. Usually the signs were simple and eye-catching, painted in bold colours, and hung outside the shop from elaborate brackets. Since communities were usually small, trades were rarely duplicated, so the signs were simple and explicit: three sugar loaves for a grocer, a goat for a dairy, a boy carrying a basket of loaves for a bakery, a boy being caned for the local schoolmaster!

What about inn signs?

Inn signs were different. Since even small communities usually had many inns, each had to have a different and distinctive sign. Also, though the erection of signs was optional for shopkeepers, from the 14th century in England inn keepers were compelled by law to erect a sign outside their premises. The great variety of inn names grew over the years, with many still surviving from early times and, though nowadays many inns and pubs are neon-lit, the traditional signs are still to be seen everywhere.

Early inn signs had a religious significance, as inns served as hostels for pilgrims on their way to Canterbury, hence The Pilgrim's Rest.

Inns called The Lamb and Flag take their name from old signs that depicted the Lamb of God, a device used by soldiers who fought in the Crusades. The Saracen's Head also commemorates the Crusades.

The still-popular Cat and Fiddle sign has nothing to do with cats—or fiddles. A brave knight who fought for France was dubbed Sir Caton le Fidele, or Sir Caton the Faithful. Inn signs were erected in his honour, but the French words were corrupted over the ages to Cat and Fiddle.

Inn signs often commemorated important historical events. The Royal Oak commemorates Charles II who, after the battle of Worcester, is said to have hidden in an oak tree.

The traditional Five Alls sign depicts a king ('I rule all'), a soldier ('I fight for all'), a farmer ('I pay for all'), a priest ('I pray for all') and a lawyer ('I plead for all').

The Cat and Kittens alludes to the large and small pewter tankards in which beer was served. Stealing these tankards was called 'cat and kitten sneaking'. Inns of this name nowadays usually carry a sign depicting a feline cat and its kittens.

GREAT COMPOSERS

Hector Berlioz

Born: Cote-St-Andre, France, December 11 1803
Died: Paris, France, March 8 1869

Berlioz was a romantic and a rebel. Although his greatest love was music, his father, a doctor, persuaded him to take up medicine by bribing him with a silver flute. But this didn't last long. Soon Berlioz announced that he intended to become a composer, and when his family disowned him he made a living by singing in a chorus.

Meanwhile he studied at the famed Paris Conservatoire and went on to teach there, with some of his own new ideas about music thrown in.

He learnt a lot about the orchestra and his 'ideal' for performances of his own *Requiem* was 242 strings, 62 woodwind instruments, 47 brass, 30 harps, 8 pairs of kettledrums, a percussion section of 47 men and a chorus of at least 360 people—a grand scale by anyone's standards!

Berlioz was also a brilliant conductor and augmented his income by writing about music as well. He married twice, but had a troubled love life and when his second wife died in 1862, followed by his son five years later, he seemed to lose the will, and died soon afterwards.

Modest Mussorgsky

Born: Karevo, Russia, March 21 1839
Died: St Petersburg, Russia, March 25 1881

Mussorgsky was once described as 'a cuckoo in a nest of singing birds' for his refusal to submit to convention and his resulting rough and uncompromising compositions.

In his opera *Boris Godunoff* his crashing chords and striking arias rang out against tyranny, seeking justice for the masses. Although now considered the perfect Russian opera it was then considered a subversive work, and it really only became a success after Mussorgsky's death.

His most famous work is his *Pictures At An Exhibition* but he also wrote other pianoforte and orchestral works as well as a number of songs noted for their simple everyday language and their basic humanity and championing of the underdog.

His own life was not always happy. Becoming depressed about living on his own, he turned to drink and, losing his friends and his money, he died a rather pathetic figure at the age of only forty-two.

Johannes Brahms

Born: Hamburg, Germany, May 7 1833
Died: Vienna, Austria, April 3 1897

Brahms used to rise every day at 5 am, make himself some strong coffee, and then begin his work, going over and over his pieces painstakingly until he was quite satisfied they were finished.

He would sometimes get discouraged. On his fiftieth birthday, for instance, he was determined to write a symphony but could think of no ideas. "I am too old to compose any more," he said and went off to his birthday dinner. Then, in a better mood, he suddenly found himself singing a melody—the melody, as it turned out, to his *Third Symphony*.

"A genius—a musical prophet," was how his fellow composer Robert Schumann described him, and he and his wife Clara were among Brahms' best friends. Indeed when Schumann died, it was to Brahms that Clara turned, and they grew very close.

Brahms was to remain a bachelor, however. "It is as hard to marry," he once said, "as it is to write an opera." He never wrote an opera either, but was to compose a huge variety of other great works.

Franz Liszt

Born: Raiding, Hungary, October 22 1811
Died: Bayreuth, Germany, July 13 1886

When he was only a few weeks old, Franz Liszt was so small and weak that his father had him measured for a coffin. But as it happened this great composer was to live life to the full, and to the tune of seventy-four years.

When asked to write the story of his life, he replied: "No, thanks, it was hard enough to have lived it." And yet success for him came without having to struggle.

He played his first public concert at the age of nine and was only eleven when Beethoven, hearing him play, told him: "You are one of the fortunate ones, for you will give joy and happiness to many people."

This Liszt did, as composer, pianist, showman and conductor. He also raised huge sums of money through benefit concerts for needy causes, and championed the 'music of the future', helping Wagner and Berlioz among many others.

TRUE OR FALSE?

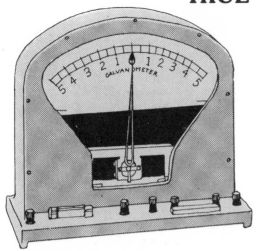

The Galvanometer was named after an Italian anatomist

Although it may seem unlikely that an instrument used to detect and measure electric current should be named after a man working with living organisms, it is in fact true. Luigi Galvani (1737-98) was the pioneer of electrophysiology—the study of the connection between living organisms and electricity—and it was his work on the muscles in frogs that led to the study of what is termed *animal electricity*.

Galvanism, a sort of electricity developed by the action of various metals and chemicals upon each other, is also named after Galvani. Iron and steel are both *galvanised* with a coating of zinc in a process known also as electroplating; it is this which helps to protect them against corrosion.

Eugenics was named after Sir Eugene Galton

The truth is that eugenics, the science of race improvement through breeding, was not named after any person; it was given its name by a Sir *Francis* Galton, whose work on heredity had led him to urge for improvement of the human race by selecting parents only from the superior classes.

Galton (1822-1911), a cousin of Charles Darwin, was also known for his work in other fields. He introduced the idea of anticyclones into meteorology; made the discovery that fingerprint patterns remain unaltered throughout life—which led to their present use for the purposes of identification—and received a gold medal from the Royal Geographical Society for his work as an anthropologist, studying the peoples of the Sudan and south-western Africa.

FRANCIS GALTON

Galilee was named after the astronomer Galileo Galilei

Since Galileo was only born in 1564, while the name Galilee dates back to over 700 years before the birth of Christ, this cannot possibly be true. The name in fact comes from the Hebrew word *galil*, meaning circle, and it is thought that this is because the Hebrews living in the Galilee area of Israel at the time were surrounded by Gentiles who had moved into the surrounding areas after the fall of Samaria in 722 BC.

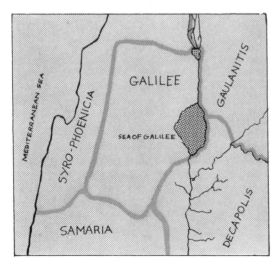

SKIN

What is Skin?

The skin is the largest and most versatile organ in the body. It is also the heaviest, weighing between 6½ and 7lbs. Basically, the skin consists of two layers, with the epidermis on the outside and the dermis underneath. New skin cells are being produced continually, and as the old ones die they are worn away from the skin's surface.

What is its function?

The skin has several functions. It protects the underlying tissue from injury and infection, it regulates the body temperature, it is a sense organ and it produces vitamin D when exposed to sunlight.

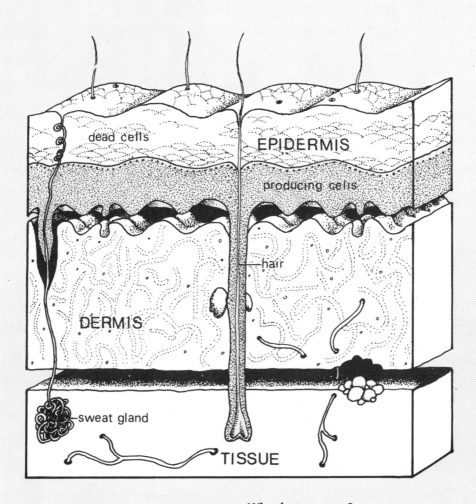

What is Goose Flesh?

Goose flesh is the name we give to the tiny bumps that appear on the skin when we are cold. The reason for it lies in the hairs that cover the skin. Air trapped between hair becomes an insulator, and the more the hair sticks out the more the trapped air and therefore the better the insulation. When the body is cold, a tiny muscle at the base of each hair contracts, making the hair stand on end and producing goose-pimples.

Why do we sweat?

Sweating is the body's most effective way of reducing its temperature. Sweat glands are situated in the dermis – there are between two and three million in most people – and they are tiny coiled tubes which open onto the skin through small holes, or pores. When the body is too hot the glands produce sweat – a mixture of water and waste products – and as it evaporates from the skin's surface it uses heat from the body, thus cooling it down. On a hot day as much as three pints of sweat are produced, mainly from the soles of the feet, the palms of the hands, under the arms and the forehead.

TALL – BUT TRUE – STORIES!

More than fifty years ago quack dentists, often dressed as Red Indians, pulled out teeth and did simple repairs in the market squares of small towns. They made sure they were accompanied by a loud brass band – to hide the screams of the customers!

In an American town police charged a man with illegal parking – after a train had demolished his car. He had left it on a level crossing!

There was a bank robbery in London when two men grabbed a jewellery shop manager's briefcase and made off. They were unlucky, though; all the briefcase contained was the manager's lunch!

Builders in Frankfurt, Germany, filled in the only doorway in a building with concrete, trapping themselves inside. They had to be rescued through a ceiling sky-light window!

In Death Valley, California, rocks are seen to move all by themselves. This is one of the many of Nature's mysteries which no-one can unravel. They can move fair distances and leave tracks behind them in the sand. Locally they are known as the 'racetrack rocks'.

A Japanese journalist was supposed to be covering a sporting event which was televised. He fell asleep half-way through – and appeared on TV! His boss was watching, and fired him!

ONE GOOD TURN . . .

There are several odd friendships in the animal world, some of which benefit the animal partners in unusual ways. Do you know:

Why the honeyguide and the ratel are friends?

The African honeyguide, as its name suggests, can quickly find a bee's nest with its delicious supply of honey. But because it is a small bird it cannot get the honey out because it fears the stings of the bees. So off he goes to tell the ratel of his find and the ratel goes off and breaks open the nest, his fur protecting him from the bees' anger. When the ratel has eaten all he wishes, there is still plenty left for the little honeyguide as a reward for finding the nest in the first place.

How does the blackbird plover help the African crocodile?

The African crocodile is a very fierce-looking creature, but the little blackbird plover does not seem in the least afraid of him. Indeed, the plover performs a great service to the crocodile by picking out the morsels of food from between the crocodile's teeth. Then this bird-toothpick eats the scraps of food himself!

In what part of the world does a woodpecker nest in the side of an ants' nest?

When the time comes for a Southern Rufous woodpecker which lives in Ceylon and India to build a nest, instead of building a nest in a tree it searches for a colony of Black Tree ants. Now normally these little insects resent intruders, but for some strange reason they allow the Rufous woodpecker to lay its eggs in a hole in the side of their ants' nest and share their home.

Why are hornbills called 'Monkey Birds'?

Hornbills get their curious nickname from the fact that they always like to be near the Guenon monkeys of the Upper African Congo when the monkeys climb the fruit trees in search of a juicy meal. The clever hornbills realise that as the monkeys pick the fruit for themselves they also discover various moths and beetles and other insects among the leaves. As these tasty insect morsels fall to the ground they are eagerly seized by the monkey bird hornbills who are delighted to be given such an easy meal from the monkeys.

Why are ostriches and zebras often seen together?

This animal-bird partnership is based on the fact that the ostrich has poor hearing and sense of smell while the zebra's two senses are highly developed, and so the zebra warns the ostrich of any nearby danger. However, the zebra's eyesight is not as keen as that of its feathered friend, the ostrich, which has really excellent eyesight especially over a distance, and the ostrich uses this eye sense to warn the zebra of any danger approaching from a distance.

One good turn, in fact . . .

HOW?

How does a Spider spin its web?

The spider's web is made of silk, which the spider produces from special glands in its abdomen. The actual spinning organ is at the tip of the abdomen and it contains many small holes. The silk is forced through these holes as a liquid, but as soon as it comes into contact with the air it hardens.

One of the most highly-developed webs is that of the garden spider. This is circular in shape, with a central zig-zag crossing the main strands for extra support.

There are hundreds of types of web, the most common being the wheel type. Other shapes include flat sheets, funnels and domes. The trap-door spider even spins a lid on its web to catch and hold its prey.

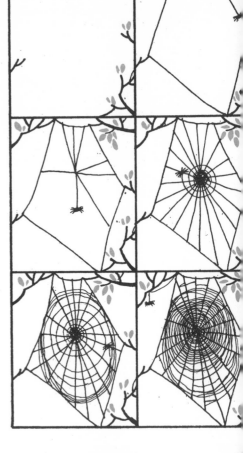

How do Oysters make pearls?

The body of an oyster is very soft and tender, and although it is protected by its shell, it also secretes a lining of mother-of-pearl to make the inside smooth.

If an irritant, such as a grain of sand, gets into the shell, the oyster immediately covers it with layer after layer of mother-of-pearl. The result is a pearl.

To speed up the process, man inserts a piece of sand or mother-of-pearl into the shell of a living oyster, and after a couple of years a pearl will have been formed. Such pearls are called 'cultured pearls' and they are cheaper to buy than the very expensive natural pearls.

How does a Weasel change colour?

Camouflage is important to many animals as a protection against their enemies. In the case of the weasel, the camouflage changes according to the season, so that during the winter, when the ground is covered with snow, its coat is white, and during the summer, brown.

The change is a gradual one, and it is triggered off by the shortening days as autumn progresses. The weasel begins to moult and as the brown hairs fall out they are replaced by white ones. By November the entire animal is white except for the black tip of its tail.

In the spring the reverse happens, although the belly of the weasel remains white all the year round.

BOOKS AND BOOKMEN

1. Who wrote *Black Beauty?*

2. In which of Charles Dickens' novels did Mr Jingle, Sam Weller and Mrs Bardell appear?

3. Under what name did Samuel L Clemens write?

4. Virginia Woolf wrote about the dog of another famous literary lady in her book *Flush*. Who was the dog's owner?

5. Mary Ann Evans wrote under a pen name; do you know it? One of her most famous books is *Silas Marner*.

6. Who wrote *Tarka the Otter* and *Salar the Salmon?*

7. Which famous writer was once known as 'Boz'?

8. Mrs Hubert Bland wrote *The Railway Children*, a very famous children's book, under a pen name. What is her pen name?

9. Who wrote *Lord Jim?*

10. What is the name of J M Barrie's famous character from Never-Never-Land?

Answers

1. Anna Sewell; 2. *The Pickwick Papers*; 3. Mark Twain; 4. Elizabeth Barratt Browning; 5. George Eliot; 6. Henry Williamson; 7. Charles Dickens; 8. E. Nesbit; 9. Joseph Conrad; 10. Peter Pan.

ORIGINS OF THE CINEMA

What is a Magic Lantern?

The magic lantern, invented in about 1660 by the Dutch physicist **Christian Huygens,** is an early version of our present day slide projector, using a strong light source which was reflected and concentrated on to a lens by a concave mirror. It was very popular throughout the 18th and 19th centuries for horror shows of ghosts and spirits, educational and travel lectures, and comic effects. Moving parts in the slides helped tell a story with 'moving pictures', and the use of several projectors simultaneously, in later years, produced a wide range of effects.

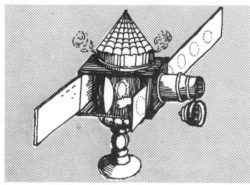

What did a Phenakistoscope do?

The phenakistoscope was the most popular of many 19th century optical toys based on the principle of *persistence of vision*, which led eventually to the creation of modern cinema. If you move a cigarette end in a rapid circle in a darkened room it appears to be a continuous circle of light, because the brain cannot distinguish all the different positions of the light at that speed. This is the phenomenon known as persistence of vision, which was first observed almost 2,000 years ago.

The phenakistoscope used a cardboard disc on which one image—for example, a horse trotting— was shown in a progressively changing series of positions. The viewer looked through the slots, one for each different picture, and saw a reflection of the image on a mirror while the disc rotated rapidly. The images seen in the mirror through the slots changed so quickly the eye interpreted it as motion.

Who first photographed motion?

Eadweard J. Muybridge, an Englishman who settled in California and became a photographer, was the first to produce a motion picture, in 1878. The main problem in producing moving pictures had been the time it was necessary for a photographic plate to be exposed; a model could stand still long enough, a moving object—by its very nature—could not.

After many years of experiment Muybridge finally succeeded in producing a set of twelve instantaneous photographs of a trotting horse and carriage, taken by twelve cameras set up in a line. Trip wires, over which the carriage passed, triggered each camera in turn, producing a series of consecutive frames which gave the appearance of motion. Muybridge went further and produced a zoopraxiscope, a more complex development of the phenakistoscope, which allowed him to project the motion picture on the screen.

Which famous inventor contributed significantly to cinema?

With the invention and development by **E.J.Marley,** between 1882 and 1890, of a single camera which could take ten photographs a second, and the introduction of flexible transparent celluloid by the American **Eastman** in 1889, the birth of the cinema was imminent. Perforations, to keep the pictures aligned with one another, were first introduced in 1890, and the need now was to invent a suitable projector to exhibit the films.

W.K.L.Dickson, a Scotsman, working in conjunction with **Thomas Edison,** produced the *kinetoscope* in 1893. This was a one-man viewing cabinet which could also be connected to the Edison phonograph to give talking pictures of a simplistic kind. One of Edison's most lasting contributions to cinema was his decision to make four perforations per frame, and to use 35mm. film, both of which are standard for cinema film even today.

When were the first public films shown?

Unfortunately for Edison he decided that his invention was a novelty which would pass off. Inspired by his work **R.W.Paul,** as well as **Birt Acres,** in England, and the **Lumière Brothers** in France, all produced their own cameras and projectors in the next two years.

The first public exhibition of moving pictures was at the **Grand Café in Paris on December 28th, 1895.** On January 14th 1896, in London, Birt Acres showed films of the Derby, the Boat Race, and the opening of the Kiel Canal. In February both the Lumières and R.W.Paul exhibited in London; by the end of the century films were being made and shown all over the world. The cinema had arrived.

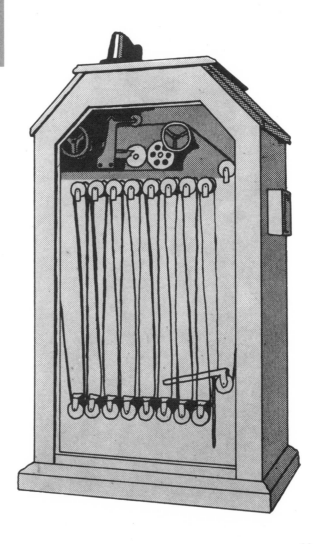

THE WORLD OF MEDICINE

What is the Hippocratic Oath?

Hippocrates, the great Greek physician, was born on the island of Cos, off the coast of Asia Minor, in about 460 B.C. His medical methods were soundly based on observation and logical reasoning, but his greatest contribution to medicine was his Oath which, although not law, still forms the basis of the ethical code or ideal for medical men.

THE HIPPOCRATIC OATH

"I will look upon him who taught me this Art even as one of my parents. I will share my substance with him, and I will supply his necessities, if he be in need. I will regard his offspring even as my own brothers, and I will teach them this Art by precept, by lecture and by every mode of teaching, not only to my own sons but to the sons of my teacher, and to disciples bound by covenant and oath, according to the Law of Medicine, but to none others.

"I will follow that method of treatment which, according to my ability and judgement, I consider for the benefit of my patients, and not for their hurt or any wrong. I will give no deadly drug to any, though it be asked of me, nor will I counsel such, and especially I will not aid a woman to procure abortion.

"Whatsoever house I enter, I will go into for the benefit of the sick, refraining from all wrong doing or corruption, and especially from any act of seduction, of male or female, of bond or free. Whatsoever things I see or hear concerning the life of men, in my attendance on the sick or even apart therefrom, which ought not to be spoken abroad, I will keep silence thereon, counting such things as sacred secrets."

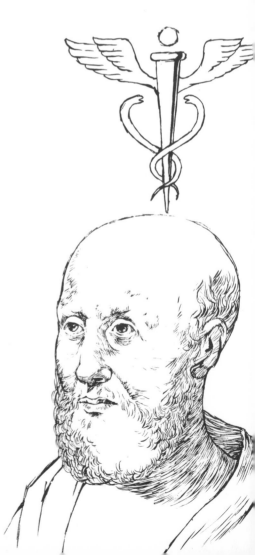

What was the Black Death?

The worst epidemic known to mankind was the Black Death which killed an estimated 75,000,000 people during its most serious outbreak in 1347-51. Originating in the ports of the Black Sea, it reached Italy, and spread throughout Europe.

The infectious organism was **Bacillus Pestis,** transmitted to man by fleas from the black rat. It caused a sudden onset of chills, fever, headaches and body pains, black or pink swellings known as *buboes*, madness and almost certain death. Approximately one in three Europeans died.

Outbreaks of the black death—whether bubonic, pneumonic, or septicaemic plague—ravaged Europe recurrently until the late 17th century. Although virtually unknown today, isolated cases still occur.

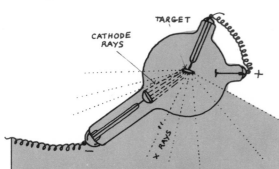

What connection is there between television and X-rays?

Wilhelm Konrad Roentgen (1845-1923) accidentally discovered X-rays in 1895, while experimenting with a Crookes tube, a glass cylinder containing two electrodes in a vacuum; when high voltage was passed through it, **cathode rays** emanated from the negative terminal.

Roentgen discovered that when these rays hit the positive terminal, the electrons inside its atoms were forced out of position and fell back into place, producing an electromagnetic wave whose rays would pass through almost any material—*unlike* cathode rays. He called them x-rays as x is used scientifically to represent the unknown.

X-rays are used widely nowadays in medicine, scientific research and industry. The cathode ray tube is, of course, part of every television set.

Which was the first disease to be defeated by vaccination?

During the 18th century 60,000,000 Europeans died of **smallpox,** yet today the disease is rare, thanks to a principle advanced by Dr. Edward Jenner (1749-1823).

Ancient country lore said that contraction of *cowpox* (transmitted from cows to humans through sores on the udders during milking) prevented smallpox. Jenner investigated thoroughly, and on 14 May 1796 innoculated an eight-year-old boy with cowpox, producing a mild illness. Later he injected him with smallpox, which was successfully resisted.

Vaccination the injecting of material which causes formation of antibodies and resultant immunity, has since been used to prevent such diseases as cholera, polio and typhoid.

THE STORY OF RUBBER

Where was rubber first found?

In South America. No one is sure who discovered it, but it is known that the Aztecs made rubber balls and even had a god of ball games called Xolotl.

The first recorded reference of rubber being heard of in Europe is a story of a French explorer who came across rubber trees being tapped in Peru in 1735.

When was it first used as an eraser?

The first recorded instance is again from the mid-18th century. Some pieces of crude rubber from South America were received by a British merchant, but he thought it useless and passed it on to his children to play with. They in turn gave a piece to a boy called Joseph Priestley who, it is said, then accidentally discovered its use as an eraser.

In 1823 the Scot Charles Macintosh found a way of using naphtha and rubber together, and thus invented waterproof cloth. Previous attempts at inventing a suitable rubberized cloth had failed since apart from being sticky, smelly and unpleasant to wear, the clothing melted if one stood near to a fire!

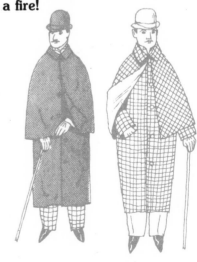

Who were the 'rubber barons'?

This is the name given to the greedy men who exploited the demand for rubber when it first came to be used as a raw material important in the manufacture of waterproofing, tyres, etc., at the beginning of this century.

At the time, all of the world's rubber came from the Amazonian forests and it was here that the 'rubber barons' set up villas and estates where they used native labour to tap the trees. They made great fortunes in no time at all, but in the process destroyed many trees and exploited a great number of people.

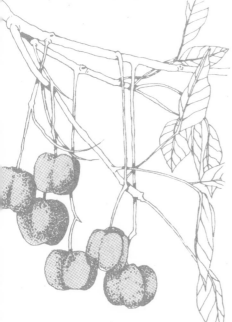

Where is rubber obtained from now?

It no longer comes from South America, for the simple reason that cheaper rubber is now being produced elsewhere. This is because an Englishman managed to smuggle some rubber tree seeds out of Brazil in 1876, cultivating them in Kew Gardens, London, and then sending some to Ceylon.

The Far East provided ideal conditions, so much so that the success of the plants there meant the end of the boom in Brazil, and therefore of the 'rubber barons'.

Now Malaya is the largest producer, with Thailand, Indonesia and Ceylon also figuring heavily. But today it is possible also to make good synthetic rubber—an invention of the Americans during the Second World War when rubber was scarce—and as this is cheaper to make than real rubber, there is more of it being produced.

Charles Goodyear, the American inventor whose name is now used for a sort of tyre, was the man responsible for the process of 'vulcanising' raw rubber. The dry rubber produced from the latex tapped from a rubber tree is soft and flexible and so unsuited to use in tyres, shoe soles, etc. Goodyear discovered that heating the raw substance with sulphur hardened it, and this invention of 1839 is still used today.

A-Z QUIZ

Question: What is an Abigail?

Answer: A lady's maid.

Question: The Gloucestershire home of the Dukes of Beaufort gave its name to a game. Can you name it?

Answer: Badminton.

Question: What is the name of a song sung in Trinidad, often to the accompaniment of steel bands?

Answer: Calypso.

Question: What was 'Dagger Money'?

Answer: The sum once paid to judges on the legal Circuit to purchase weapons as a protection against robbers.

Question: Which country has the white-headed eagle as its emblem?

Answer: The United States of America.

Question: Who wrote *The Fair Maid of Perth*?

Answer: Sir Walter Scott.

Question: Who is the god of war, according to ancient Rome?

Answer: Mars.

Question: In heraldry, what colour is *gules*?

Answer: Red.

Question: Who has the motto: *Ich Dien*?

Answer: The Prince of Wales.

Question: Who wrote about the Jabberwocky?

Answer: Lewis Carroll.

Question: What is a 'Kentucky Pill'?

Answer: A bullet.

Question: Where is the 'Land of the White Eagle'?

Answer: Poland.

Question: What does MS stand for?

Answer: Manuscript.

Question: What is a Naiad?

Answer: A water nymph.

Question: Who hid from his enemies in an oak tree?

Answer: Charles II.

Question: What is a palindrome?

Answer: A word which reads the same when read either backwards or forwards.

Question: What is another name for Quicksilver?

Answer: Mercury.

Question: What name is given to the sign of the ram in the zodiac?

Answer: Aries.

Question: Who is the patron saint of travellers?

Answer: St. Christopher.

Question: What is the 'Third Estate'?

Answer: The House of Commons.

Question: Who was the first person to use an umbrella in Britain?

Answer: Jonas Hanway.

Question: By what name is Van Dieman's Land now known?

Answer: Tasmania.

Question: What is wampum?

Answer: Shell bead money used by the North American Indians.

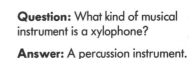

Question: What kind of musical instrument is a xylophone?

Answer: A percussion instrument.

Question: What is the song of the Yellowhammer?

Answer: "A little bit of bread and no cheese."

Question: What are the Zingari?

Answer: This is the name given to gypsies in Italy.

WOULD YOU BELIEVE IT?

Amazing facts about exotic pets in history . . .

A story straight out of the Arabian Nights – but perfectly true – is about Zureyk the blue-eyed lion, who was the pet of Sultan Khumaraweyh of Cairo, many hundreds of years ago. Zureyk would guard his master's side through the day and night. The Sultan suffered from insomnia, so he would while away the hours lying on an air-bed in a pool of quicksilver, listening to tame turtle doves singing in the trees. Zureyk lay in a bed of roses.

The Romans loved having exotic pets, too. Elegabalus, a dissipated Emperor, used his lions as rather fierce practical jokers! After inviting guests to a dinner party at which they ate and drank too much, Elegabalus let his lions into the room while they were recovering from their stupor. Not a pleasant way to be revived!

Other Romans in high places dressed Barbary apes in rich togas and trained them to play musical instruments at gala occasions. They seemed to enjoy the apes' music!

Legend tells, in China, that once a lion and a marmoset fell in love. Because the lion is very large while the marmoset is very small, a Buddhist monk took pity on them and shrank the lion to the marmoset's size. Out of this union came the Pekinese dog – which, Chinese people believe, has the heart and courage of a lion within its small body.

When British and French soldiers broke into the Forbidden City of Peking in 1860 they found the dead Empress of China fiercely guarded by her faithful Pekinese dogs. Although they fought bravely, their small size was against them and they were taken as bounty. One ended up in the Royal Court of Queen Victoria!

SOUND: WHAT IS IT?

What is an oscilloscope?

It is an electronic device which enables one to 'see sound'. Sounds are made by something vibrating, and so making the air around it vibrate. The motion of the vibrating object, back and forwards, compresses the air and then allows it to expand again, and this is repeated with each vibration. This in turn affects the air further from the object, such that the vibration travels through the air in all directions, until it eventually dies away. These vibrations are known as *sound waves*, and an oscilloscope shows the pattern, or shape, of these waves on a screen similar to a TV screen. The sound is fed into the machine through a microphone, which changes the energy of the sound waves into electrical energy, as an electric current.

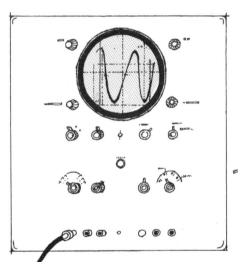

What is the speed of sound?

It is much slower than the speed of light (186,282 miles a second) and depends upon the density and elasticity of the medium through which the sound is travelling. The denser the medium, the slower it moves; the more elastic, the faster it moves. The speed is about 16400 feet a second in steel, 4700 f.p.s. in water, and 1100 f.p.s. in air at 0°C (32°F). The large difference between the speed of light and sound give one method of determining how far you are from thunder and lightning, since you will see the lightning before you hear the clap of thunder. The lightning will be about a mile away for every five seconds counted between the two.

What is meant by supersonic speed?

These are speeds faster than the speed of sound. Jet planes often fly at these speeds – Concorde, for example, is designed to fly at 2.2 times the speed of sound.

When the plane reaches the speed of sound, it has reached the *sound barrier*, a resistance in the air which the aircraft must break through. In fact, it slices through the 'solid' air, as if cutting with a knife, and the nose of the plane produces a shock wave (or *bow wave*), while its rear end creates vacuum.

Air rushing in to fill this vacuum causes turbulence called a *vortex path*.

The bow wave spreads out, and forms the shape of a cone, and it is where this cone meets up with the ground, that the noise of the jet is heard. If the aircraft is below 30,000 feet, the sound pressure may rise as high as 30lb. per square feet, enough to shatter windows. This phenomenon is known as a *sonic bang*.

In aviation, the speed of an aircraft at any time can be given by a *Mach number*, the ratio of that speed to the speed of sound in the air through which it is flying, and named after the Austrian physicist Ernst Mach (1838–1916).

Mach 0.5 is half the speed of sound, or *subsonic*.
Mach 1 is the speed of sound, or *transonic*.
Mach 2 is twice the speed of sound, or *supersonic*.

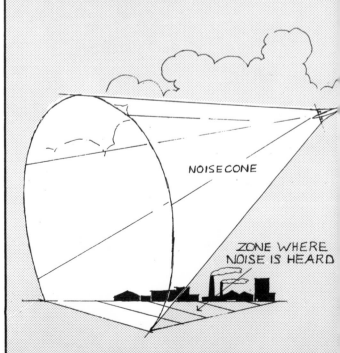

NOISE CONE

ZONE WHERE NOISE IS HEARD

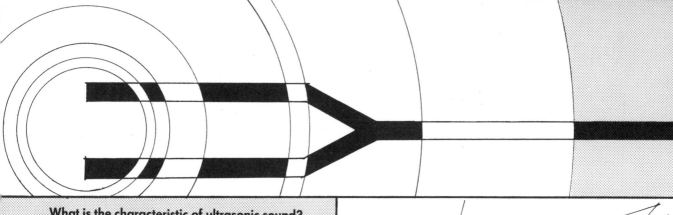

What is the characteristic of ultrasonic sound?

It vibrates at frequencies too high for the human ear to hear, i.e. anything over 20,000 times a second. Ultrasonic waves can be focussed like the beam from a searchlight, and the beam's reflection can easily be detected.

On this basis, naval vessels use ultrasonic devices (called *sonars*) for detecting submarines under water, by listening for echoes reflected from them. Devices to measure the depth of the ocean, or to locate schools of fish, are two more examples.

Ultrasonic waves are also used to detect flaws, for example weaknesses in railway lines; to kill insects; to pasteurise milk; to sterilise surgical instruments, and to treat arthritis. And an ultrasonic drill can be used on both metals and teeth, where it is less painful than drills which are not ultrasonic, and which can be heard by the patient as well as felt!

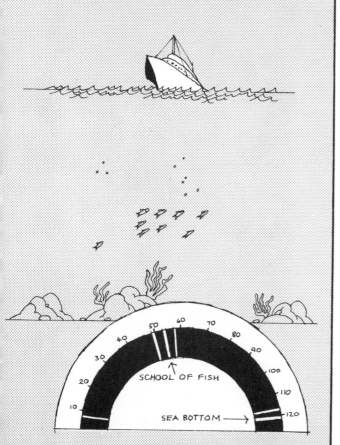

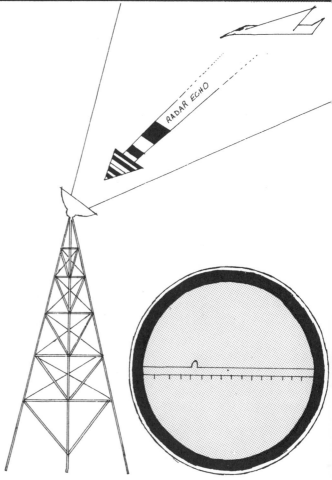

Which ultrasonic sound is an elementary form of radar?

The high-pitched twittering of the bat. The pitch of this sound is a lot higher than a human can hear, but bats use it to warn of impending obstacles, by listening for the echoes of their twittering, as the ultrasonic sound bounces off a house, a tree, a person or whatever.

Radar – which stands for **R**adio **D**irection **A**nd **R**ange – works by the use of a very high power pulse of radio energy, at a speed of about 186,000 miles per second. The radar echoes picked up by the radio receiver are shown on an oscilloscope, and the distance of the object is measured using electronic circuits, while the direction is determined by a *directional antenna*.

ALL AT SEA

What is a 'Hippocampus'?

This word is derived from two Greek words meaning horse and sea monster, and therefore it is another name for a seahorse, that strange little creature which is sometimes used as the model for a knight in the game of chess.

The seahorse has a long snout and prominent eyes and a tail by which he clings tightly to a piece of seaweed. The seahorse swims in an upright position using his dorsal fin and is carried along by the strong ocean currents. He feeds on tiny living sea creatures which he sucks into his mouth as he swims along . . . and it is the male seahorse who looks after the eggs, in a special pouch under his body, until they are safely hatched out!

Who was the 'Shantyman'?

The Shantyman was the sailor who sang the solo lines in a sea shanty while the rest of the ship's crew sang the remaining chorus lines. Sea shanties were a way of getting men to work together efficiently when performing tasks aboard the old time sailing ships. On certain lines in the shanty the men would push or pull together.

Windlass and *halliard* were two kinds of sea shanties. The former, also known as a *capstan* shanty, was used for weighing anchor, while the *halliard* was used for hauling up sails.

Who sailed in the Longships?

The Scandinavian sea warriors known as the Vikings sailed the North Atlantic and the Baltic and Mediterranean Seas in longboats which had one sail and which used oars as power. A longship was about eighty feet long, hence its name, and almost seventeen feet in width. The ships were very shallow and there were some thirty or forty Vikings to a ship. These men could sail in almost any sea because their longships were so well constructed.

The Danish Vikings raided and plundered England, France and Spain, the Swedish Vikings raided Germany while the Norwegian Vikings in their horned helmets travelled to Greenland, Iceland, Ireland and Scotland, and became the subjects of many colourful heroic sagas.

What is a group of seals called?

A group of seals is called a *pod*. Seals are warm-blooded animals which live in the sea but which gather in a *rookery* to breed. Female seals are called *cows* and their offspring *pups* or *calves*. True seals have no outer ears, they just have holes at the side of their heads, while sea-lions and fur seals make up one of the families known as the eared seals. Walruses are distinguished from other seals by their large tusks.

Common seals are found in Europe and North America, large Elephant seals in northern and southern waters, while Greenland seals live in North Atlantic and Arctic oceans. The ferocious Leopard seals live in the Antarctic, while the rare Grey seals live in the waters around the British Isles.

Although fur-seal hunting is strictly controlled, Eskimoes hunt seals for food, using the seals' skins for the roofs of their summer homes and for making shoes and clothing for themselves and their families.

Do any snakes live in the sea?

There are nearly fifty different kinds of sea snakes, all with one exception living in waters between the Persian Gulf and Polynesia. The Yellow-bellied Sea Snake lives in Africa and Mexico.

Sea snakes, such as the one illustrated here with its black rings or bars on its blue body, belong to the *Hydropphidae* family. It has a wide tail which it uses as an oar when swimming, and although it comes to the surface to breathe it can dive to great depths to catch its fishy food.

Female snakes hatch out their eggs on a sandy beach and all the sea snakes are far more poisonous than their land cousins – so beware!

EDWARD LEAR AND CHARLES DICKENS

Edward Lear and Charles Dickens both lived during the last century, but their work was very different – just as their lives were. Yet we remember them both today with affection and respect.

Edward Lear

Edward Lear was born in Highgate, London, in 1812, and he was only one of twenty-one children! His childhood must have been fascinating, if a little crowded; his parents employed a fleet of servants and owned no less than twelve carriages.

At the age of thirteen, though, Edward Lear's father lost much of his wealth and the large family had to break up. Edward went to live with his sister Ann, of whom he was very fond. She taught him at home, as he wasn't well enough to go to school, and one of his favourite hobbies was drawing wild-life and plants.

As he grew up this interest became his career, and his first job was to draw the parrots at London Zoo! This took him a year and after this he was invited by the Earl of Derby to live in his stately home near Liverpool in order to draw the Earl's private menagerie. Edward stayed there for four years, and during this time met many famous and rich people, but he liked to be with the Earl of Derby's children best of all, and it was for them that he first made up his 'nonsense' poems.

Edward didn't think of himself as a poet, however. He always considered himself to be an artist, and after his work for the Earl was finished he travelled around the world, drawing everything he saw. This life wasn't always easy as Edward was often ill, sad and poor, but he went on drawing and writing his funny verses. He never married or raised any children, but thousands of children all over the world are enchanted by his strange poems.

Charles Dickens

Charles Dickens must have had a very different childhood from Edward Lear's. Charles was sticking labels on bottles in a miserable factory while Edward would probably have been playing with some of his many toys. Charles Dickens' father was often in debt; Charles often went to see his parents in debtors' prison at Marshalsea. The experience affected him deeply and he wrote about it in some of his later books.

His father's fortunes did change later, though, and Charles was able to go to school, then become an office boy to a solicitor. He was much happier, and during this time began to write and draw sketches, using his nickname 'Boz'. It wasn't long before 'Boz' became well-known, and Dickens had a great success with his *Pickwick Papers*. He used his memories of prison for this book, then went on to write of his boyhood in his next novel *David Copperfield*. He had gained this writing expertise by becoming a reporter for a London paper, and from this early success, went on to write many masterful books.

After seeing so much of the darker side of life himself, Dickens was very anxious that people should know about the injustices of Victorian England, especially against children.

He exposed the way that young boys were encouraged to steal in packs, led by a cruel master, in *Oliver Twist*, and the fraudulent and harsh 'schools' set up for boys away from home, in *Nicholas Nickleby*. In fact, this book helped to close such schools down.

Charles Dickens married while he was quite young, and had many friends during his life. He toured America a number of times; Americans loved his tales of London life as much as the British did! He died in 1870.

RELIGIONS OF THE WORLD

Try this quiz and find out how much you know about the different religions of the world.

1. Buddhism is the Western name for the teachings of an Indian prince. Do you know his name?

2. Do you know which religion has the Koran as its holy book?

3. In Japan there was once a form of ancestor worship. Do you know what it was called?

4. A great Chinese philosopher and sage began a cult, which later became a religion when his followers regarded him as a God. Do you know what he was called?

5. Do you know what a *stupa* is?

6. Do you know what litanies are?

7. Do you know what the ceremony of 'bar-mitzvah' is about, and to which religion it belongs?

8. Do you know what Church Archbishop Makarios was the head of?

Check your answers on page 191

THE LOST PEOPLE: THE AZTECS

Who were the Aztecs?

They were ancient American Indians who lived in Mexico from A.D. 1200 until the coming of Cortés in 1521. The Aztec Indians created a highly advanced and powerful form of civilisation. They built large and well-planned cities, and had organised governments.

In appearance, they were sturdy people with dark skins and straight, dark hair; in fact very like the Indians who still live around Mexico. Most of the Aztecs spoke the *Nahuatl* language, from which we have taken such words as tomato, chili and chocolate.

What was the Aztecs' religion?

The Aztecs worshipped many gods, usually in the form of animals. Their beliefs were so strong that religion dominated even civil laws and decisions. The Aztecs waged war on other peoples not only because of political reasons, but to bring back prisoners of war. Rather a gruesome element in the Aztecs religion was the human sacrifice of these prisoners, often in the most barbaric ways. Alongside the temples in the plaza would stand racks of thousands of severed heads, evidence of the sacrifices.

The favourite Aztec god was *Huitzilopochtli*, or Hummingbird Wizard, god of war and of the sun. There were many others: *Quetzalcoatl*, the Plumed Serpent, is the most important, the god of learning and of the priesthood.

How did they live?

Outside the cities, the Aztec Indians lived in simple houses made of *adobe* (mud bricks) with a thatched roof. The husband worked in the fields while the wife ground corn and made unleavened cakes called *tortillas*. They would also spin and weave cloth.

Clothes were made from the fibres of the century plant. Men wore loin-cloths, capes and sandals, while women wore short skirts and sleeveless blouses. Many of their clothes were beautifully decorated, and the designs indicated the wearer's position in society.

The chief city of the Aztecs, *Tenochtitlán*, was built where the modern Mexico City stands today. The Spanish explorer Cortés called the city 'The Venice of the New World', as it was built up from the bed of the Lake Texcoco. The city was a wonder of ancient engineering: as well as many canals there were also aqueducts, causeways and movable drawbridges. All the main canals and roadways led to the main plaza or square, where many temples dedicated to the Aztec gods stood. The main government buildings were situated there as well.

Were the Aztecs great craftsmen?

They are famous all over the world for their work with precious metals like gold and silver. They carved many fine pieces of jewellery from jade, and dyed cloth in the most beautiful designs. They made pottery, and sculpted in stone.

The most famous Aztec sculpture is the Aztec Calendar Stone, twice the size of a man, showing the sun-god *Tonatiuh* and outlining the Aztec version of world history, myths and prophecy. They also built many temples, with stone carvings and long stairways.

Did the Aztecs have money?

No. Instead, they paid taxes and traded in food, clothing, skins, pottery, gold and silver. Taxes had to be paid to the emperor, who ruled supreme over the high council, who elected him. Only military men could attain high rank in Aztec society and all men had to serve in the army. Historians belive the Aztecs were the first Indians to use swords.

Did the Aztecs have schools?

Yes. Priests trained young girls and boys for official religious duties in special schools called *calmecacs*, and there were also *telpuchcalli* (houses of youth) where history, Aztec traditions, crafts and religious observances were taught. But the Aztecs were unable to write; they formed picture-writing symbols on books made of leaves, rolled into a scroll. Some of these survive today.

How did the Aztecs die out?

This happened when the Spanish explorer Hernando Cortés discovered the Aztec Empire in 1519. At first on good terms with the Spanish, the Aztecs were betrayed when Cortés imprisoned their emperor and, after much fighting, finally conquered the Aztecs in 1521, with the aid of horses, guns and iron weapons.

The Aztec civilisation collapsed almost immediately after this defeat. Many of the people died from European diseases brought by the Spanish. Cortés had the plaza and the temples, government buildings and the market-places levelled to the ground, building his own administration offices there.

There are still many descendants of the Aztec Indians living in small villages near Mexico City, and they speak the language of their forefathers. But most of their customs and religions are taken from the Spanish soldiers who settled in their land so many years ago.

CASTLE QUIZ

What are motte and bailey castles?

These were the earliest Norman castles. They were built on the top of a man-made mound with a ditch and a wooden fence around the 'bailey', which was an area of ground around the wooden fort used for defending the castle. The wooden buildings are gone now, of course, but it's still possible to see the mounds, or 'mottes'.

What are curtain walls?

Castles built in later years had strong curtain walls, made of stone and often very thick indeed. These walls went all around the castle and had many principal rooms built into them, usually in the shape of towers. Sometimes there would be a double circle of walls for extra security.

What are pele towers and keeps?

Pele towers are strong, fortified towers. They stand by themselves, without the moat or drawbridge of other types of castle, usually on higher ground. They can be seen near the Borders, as they were built to fight bands of marauders which used to cross into Scotland or England from their own lands to harass and steal.

Keeps are towers, too, built by the Normans when they had established a stronghold on Britain and could create permanent castles made of stone. The keep was the central tower, surrounded by battlements.

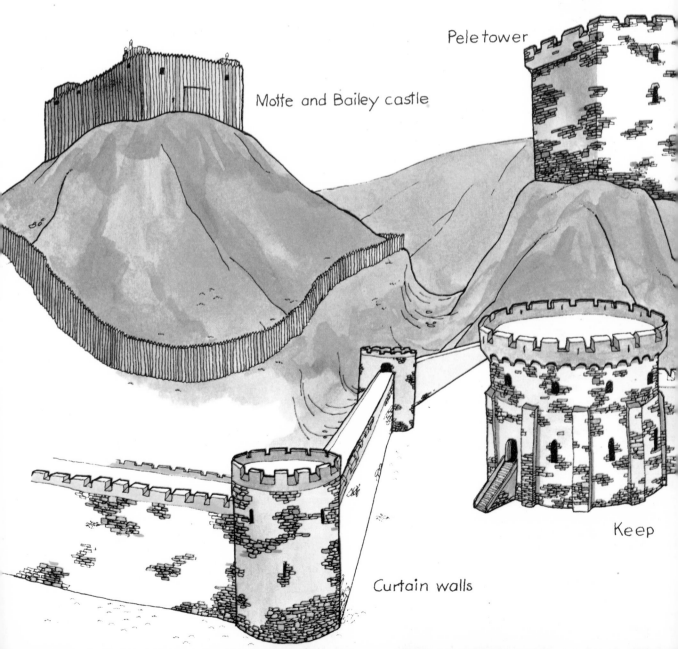

Motte and Bailey castle

Pele tower

Curtain walls

Keep

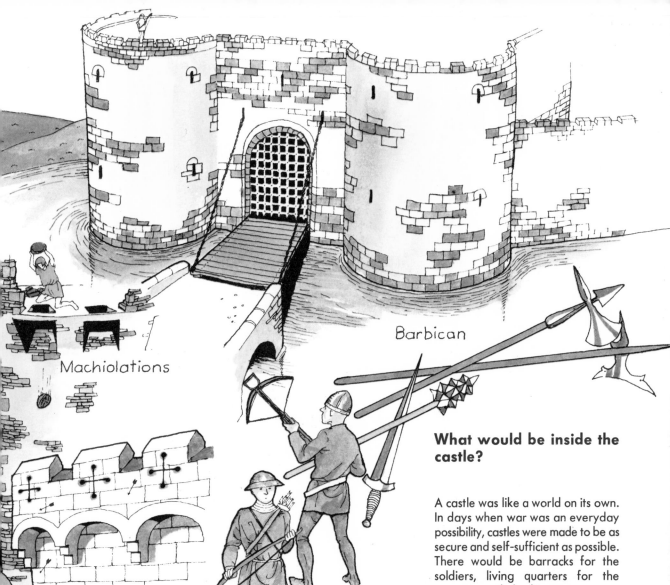

Barbican

Machiolations

What would be inside the castle?

A castle was like a world on its own. In days when war was an everyday possibility, castles were made to be as secure and self-sufficient as possible. There would be barracks for the soldiers, living quarters for the servants and the kings, queens or noblemen, as well as kitchens, wells and granaries to produce the immense amount of food needed to feed the many people living in the castle. There would be cellars for wine and stores, a great banqueting hall, quarters for the animals that would be kept for food, and stables for the horses. Most important, there would be an armoury, where weapons were kept, and areas like the barbican, where the castle would be defended. In some castles there would be a paved courtyard in the very centre, or gardens where the people would sit. There would be laundries and places where craftsmen would work, making pottery, weapons or shoeing horses. Lavatories were set into the thick outer walls of the castle and were known as garderobes.

What are machiolations?

These are long holes let into the roof from the battlements of a castle. Their use was, in centuries gone by, to protect the people inside the castle while they hurled down missiles on to the heads of the attackers. Very similar are the arrow loops you can see in many castles, let into the walls. They were for bowmen who could point their arrows through these holes without being seen themselves. Sometimes you'll see arrow loops in the shape of crosses; the horizontal slits were for archers using crossbows.

What was the barbican?

The barbican was an outer defence building in a castle, situated close to the gatehouse, where the drawbridge and portcullis were kept. Soldiers would use the barbican as an outer defence when the castle was being attacked. The portcullis was a large door made of iron or wooden bars which could be lowered or raised by way of grooves cut into the doorway. It was another defence against invaders, as was the drawbridge, which was a bridge raised or lowered on chains across the moat.

YOU AND YOUR BODY

WHAT ARE REFLEXES?

Most of the movements we make are completely under our control, but some, the *reflex actions*, are not. A reflex action is an automatic response to a stimulus, for example pain, and we cannot control it at all.

If you were to touch something very hot, your hand would automatically be pulled away before you had realised that it was burning. This is because the nerves in your hand send a message to the brain, which immediately sends back the message which pulls the hand away – all in a split second.

Other examples of reflex actions are blinking when a spec of grit gets in the eye, and the way your mouth waters when you think of certain foods.

SALT   SWEET

SOUR   BITTER

WHAT IS TASTE?

Taste is one of the five senses, the others being sight, smell, touch and hearing. Our chief organ of taste is the tongue, which is covered with tiny cells or *taste buds*. These react to different tastes and send messages to the brain.

You may be surprised to learn that there are in fact only *four* kinds of taste: sweet, sour, salty and bitter. All the flavours we know are a combination of these four.

Just as there are four kinds of taste, so there are four kinds of taste bud, and these are situated in different areas of the tongue. Only the centre of the tongue has no buds at all, as you will see if you put a little salt on the middle of your tongue. Experiment with other flavours to find the areas of taste buds on your tongue, and then see how placing an ice cube on your tongue affects your sense of taste.

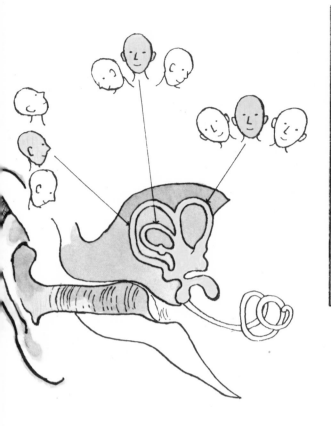

WHAT IS BALANCE?

Balance is what keeps us upright, although we tend to take it for granted unless we are standing on a swaying bus or crossing a narrow bridge. But how do we know when we are upright? The answer lies in our ears, in three small tubes called *semi-circular canals*. These canals are filled with liquid and they act very much like a spirit level. When we tip them the liquid flows to one side and bumps against special nerves which immediately send messages to the brain, telling it how far we should move to regain our balance.

There are three of these canals in each ear, although they have nothing to do with our hearing. One canal is concerned with twisting movements, one with sideways movements, and one with backward and forward movements.

HOW DO WE SMELL?

Our organ of smell is, of course, the nose, and it is the weakest of our five senses. As we breathe in air through our nostrils, any gases or tiny particles it contains are carried into the nasal cavity to the *olfactory* (smell-detecting) *nerves*. The tiny nerve endings react to the various chemicals that make up a smell, and the result is sent along the main olfactory nerve to the special reception centre in the brain.

Smell and taste are very closely associated, and often what we think of as a taste is in fact a smell. For example, coffee, tobacco, apples and potatoes are 'tasted' in the nose. To prove this, try blindfolding a friend, then hold his nose while he eats a slice of apple and a slice of potato. He will find it hard to distinguish between them.

A KINDLE OF CATS

A collection of cats is called a kindle, and here is a collection of questions on cats . . . of many kinds!

In which book does the Cheshire Cat appear?

Alice in Wonderland by Lewis Carroll. This is the story of the adventures of a little girl when she followed a White Rabbit down a hole and met such fascinating creatures and the Mad Hatter, the Queen of Hearts, the Dormouse . . . and of course, the Cheshire Cat, who had a large head and a wicked smile!

Who was Bubastis?

The Egyptian goddess with the face of a cat, to whom all cats were sacred and whom the Egyptians worshipped as the high priestess of the animals which saved their grain stores from mice.

What were the Catacombs?

The underground passages where the early Christians held services and buried their dead. It was in these passages, carved out of the soft rock, that the Christians hid when they fled for their lives from the Romans.

What was the first Catamaran?

A raft or number of logs tied side by side and longest in the middle. It was used to get to and from shore to ship on a short voyage.

What is unusual about a Manx cat?

It has no tail, because according to legend, it was so late getting to the Ark that Noah closed the door before it got inside properly . . . and so it lost its tail!

Can you give another name for the Cat-bear?

This is one of the names of the Red Panda, which has lovely red fur and lives in the Himalayas, where it feeds on fruit and leaves.

QU-QU-QUIZ

Here's a quick test on things beginning with 'qu' . . . .

1. What were quaestors?

2. What is quartz?

3. Do you know what quasars are?

4. When someone's in quarantine, what's happened to them?

5. What kind of animal is a quail?

6. Quetzal is the name of two different things. Do you know what they are?

7. What is a quince?

8. Where is the Quai d'Orsay?

Check your answers on page 191

BOOKS AND BOOKMEN

What is the Domesday Book?

This is a record, ordered to be collected by William the Conqueror, of those owning property in England, together with the amount of property they owned. The Domesday Book, which is in two volumes, was completed in 1086, and enabled William to devise a system to tax this land. One volume covered Essex, Norfolk and Suffolk while the other covered the remaining part of Anglo-Saxon England.

The Domesday Book was written in Latin and it is also known as 'The King's Book' and 'The Winchester Roll'. Today it is kept in London in the Public Records Office.

Who was William Caxton?

Caxton was known as 'The Father of English Printing' because after learning his trade in Germany and Belgium he set up his printing press 'At the sign of the Red Pale' where he printed his first book in England. It was called *The Dictes or Sayings of Philosophers*, but Caxton had already helped to produce an English translation in Flanders of *The Recuyell of the Histories of Troy* and later he published Chaucer's *Canterbury Tales* and Malory's *Le Morte d'Arthur*.

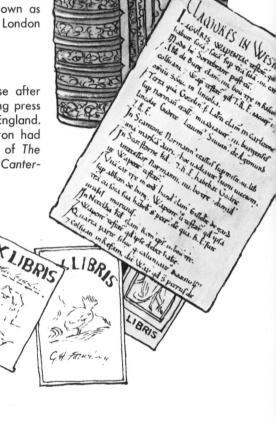

What is a 'Bookplate'?

A bookplate is a printed label which a person pastes into the front of his books to show that he owns them. Today, bookplates are coming back into fashion, some featuring birds and animals, others scenes from well-known books.

The first bookplates were made in the early 15th century in Germany. They were woodcuts, coloured by hand. Albrecht Dürer designed the first printed bookplate in the early 16th century.

Today some people collect old bookplates as a hobby. A Charles Dickens, William Wordsworth or Brönte sisters bookplate would be a treasure indeed, if you were lucky enough to find one!

Where would you see 'The Book of Kells'?

In Trinity College, Dublin. It is a beautifully illustrated manuscript of the four gospels dating back to the 8th century. It is believed that this book with its exquisite decoration and calligraphy was the work of the monks of a monastery founded by St Columba at Kells in County Meath. Because of the detail in its penmanship and elaborate borders this book is said to be the best of its kind in this field of art in early times.

SPACE SHOTS

Check your answers on page 191

Since America and Russia cut back on their manned space programmes, a lot of the public's interest in space travel has disappeared. But still there are satellites and unmanned probes visiting other planets to help us unlock the secrets of our solar system.

Just how much do you know about space?

1. Which of the planets in our solar system travels the fastest?
2. Who was the first man to be launched into space?
3. In what ship was he travelling?
4. Who discovered the planet Uranus?
5. Which planet was named after the Roman God who ruled the underworld?
6. Who first suggested that it was the sun and not the earth that was the centre of our solar system?
7. Who was the first woman in space?
8. Who was the second man to step down onto the moon?
9. Does the moon orbit the earth or the earth orbit the moon?
10. Which planet is known as the Red Planet?

THEY WERE FIRST!

Who built the first working submarine?

Although various experimental models had been produced – such as a leather-covered rowing boat which could submerge – it was not until 1775 that an American named David Bushnell built the first working submarine, which he named the *Turtle*. A year later it was used in an attempt to blow up the British warship *Eagle* during the American War of Independence. An American named Ezra Lee tried to attach a mine to the hull of the warship, but failed because the hull was encased in copper!

Who invented the first miners' safety lamp?

Sir Humphrey Davy produced his safety lamp in 1815, which protected miners from the danger of gas formed by decaying coal, known as firedamp. The safety lamp was like an oil lamp surrounded by gauze which formed a guard around the flame. If the wick was lowered, a blue flame would appear around the main flame if firedamp was present, and this would give the miner enough time to get well away from the danger area. Some safety lamps cannot be opened and others go out if opened. The Davy safety lamp has helped to save many lives.

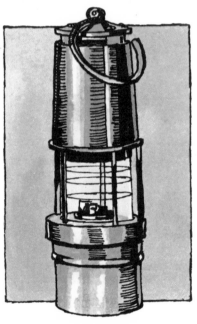

Who built the first practical working model of a sewing machine?

Although Englishman Thomas Saint patented the first sewing machine in 1790, made from wood and with a needle which had a notch and not an eye, it was a Frenchman, Barthelomy Thimonnier, who finally produced the first practical sewing machine about forty years later. He used it for making uniforms for soldiers, but he was almost killed by angry workmen who thought that this machine would deprive them of their living!

Who made the first non-stop trans-atlantic flight?

John William Alcock and Arthur Whitten Brown, who won the £10,000 prize money by flying a Royal Air Force Vickers Vimy bomber with Rolls-Royce Eagle VIII engines, from St. John's in Newfoundland to County Galway in Ireland, in May 1919. These airmen had to fight fog, instrument failure and bad storms on the journey, and for their great courage they were later knighted by King George V.

INGENIOUS INVENTIONS

The telescope was invented by Galileo, an Italian astronomer many centuries ahead of his time. As early as 1609 he had found a way of making lenses strong enough to view the heavens clearly, and he discovered that, contrary to beliefs popular at that time, the earth was not the centre of the universe! During his lifetime, despite his invention, he was ridiculed for his ideas.

The telephone was invented by Alexander Graham Bell, a teacher of the deaf. He worked hard trying to transmit the sound of a human voice through machinery, but at first his telephone could only pick up strange, blurred sounds. In 1876 the first clearly-heard and understood transmission was made by accident, when Bell cried out after spilling some acid and was heard by his assistant in another room.

The electric light was the culmination of a great deal of hard work and hope for Thomas Edison. His incandescent electric lamp was produced in 1879, a glass bulb with carbonised cotton thread connected to the source of electricity by platinum wires. The cotton threads were changed and tungsten replaced them this century, but Edison's invention meant a turning-point in the world's history.

The printing press came into being because of the ingenuity of a man called Gutenberg. His invention of movable type was probably the most important discovery of the Renaissance, and made the spread of learning far more rapid and far-reaching than if books had had to continue being hand-made and laboriously written out. It is due to Gutenberg that we are able to discover new ideas through the wide range of books available today.

ALPHABET OF FAMOUS BATTLES

Armada, 1588

The first great gun battle at sea. Lord Howard of Effingham led the English fleet in the defeat of the 130-ship *Invincible Armada* of Philip II of Spain. Drake, Hawkins and Frobisher played prominent parts in the victory.

Culloden, 1746

The battle that marked the end for Prince Charles Edward Stuart, 'Bonny Prince Charlie', in his fight to win Scotland's crown from the English. His army, made up mostly of farmers, ill-prepared for the fierce fighting, was defeated by the Duke of Cumberland on Culloden moor, near Inverness.

Dunkirk, 1940

The Germans attacked relentlessly all the time that the great evacuation of Dunkirk was taking place. This was one of the best-organised withdrawals of troops ever carried out. All kinds of vessels, from destroyers to rowing-boats, sailed to the French coast to rescue retreating Allied forces and take them to Britain.

Balaclava, 1854

The battle which included the famous 'Charge of the Light Brigade' on September 6, when the Light Cavalry was sent into action against the Russian artillery. This was a disastrous and crucial point in the Crimean War. Two hundred and fifty men were wounded from a force of about 670.

Gettysburg, 1863

The Union army defeated the Confederate forces of General Robert E. Lee when they met accidentally at Gettysburg. This marked a turning-point in the American Civil War, which heralded defeat for the South. Gettysburg is now a memorial graveyard for those who died.

Hastings, 1066

This, one of the most important battles of history, gave the Normans control of England when William, Duke of Normandy, defeated the Saxon king Harold. During the battle Harold's eye was pierced by a spear. The Bayeux tapestry commemorates the battle.

Leipzig, 1813

The battle sometimes referred to as 'The Battle of the Nations'. A combined army of Prussians, Russians and Swedes defeated Napoleon's army near Leipzig.

Jutland, 1916

This battle, the only major confrontation between Britain and Germany's main fleets in World War One, left Britain master of the seas. The British Grand Fleet was led by Admiral Jellicoe, the German Fleet led by Admiral von Scheer. The battle took place in the channel between Norway and Jutland called the Skaggerak.

Iwo Jima, 1945

This battle marked some of the bloodiest fighting during World War Two. The American Marines captured the tiny but strategically vital island of Iwo Jima from the Japanese.

Marathon, 490 B.C.

Darius's Persian army wanted to invade Greece, but was defeated by a much smaller force of Athenians and Plataeans, led by Militiades.

Stalingrad, 1942-3

The German Sixth Army captured Stalingrad from the Russians after much heavy fighting during World War Two. But Russian forces counter-attacked and sieged the Germans in the city. After a long time the Germans, under General Von Paulus, surrendered. This was the first major defeat of the Germans in Russia. Stalingrad is now called Volgograd.

Orleans, 1429

Joan of Arc led the French into battle and forced the English to end the siege of Orleans. This was a decisive battle of the Hundred Years' War.

Trafalgar, 1805

Admiral Lord Nelson led the British fleet to victory against a combined French and Spanish fleet off Cape Trafalgar on the southern coast of Spain. Nelson, on HMS Victory, lost his life in the battle, which established Britain's command of the seas.

Quebec, 1759

General Wolfe made a surprise attack on Quebec from the St. Lawrence river, where the French were besieged, and his attack was successful, although both Wolfe and the French commander Montcalm, were killed. The battle marked the end of French control in North America.

Waterloo, 1815

'The Iron Duke', Wellington, with his outnumbered armies, held off Napoleon's French forces until the arrival of Prussian reinforcements under Marshal Blucher. This meant that Napoleon suffered a crushing defeat which brought about his final downfall and exile to St. Helena.

STATUES WITH A STORY

Around the world in many countries there are many interesting statues, some of which have an unusual story behind them.

The Statue of Liberty towers some 305 feet high over Liberty Island, off the channel of New York harbour. The people of France gave this symbol of 'Liberty Enlightening the World' to the United States of America in 1884, in commemoration of the centenary of the American War of Independence. The statue, which is of bronze, had as its model Mme Tallien, 'Notre-Dame-de-Thermidor', and is the work of an Alsatian sculptor named Auguste Bartholdi.

In Rome there is a bronze statue of two small boys being fed by a she-wolf. The children are Romulus and Remus, the legendry founders of the city, who were the sons of Mars and Rhea Sylvia. Left to die, they were found and fed by the wolf and they grew to manhood. The brothers planned to build a great city, but they quarrelled about this and in a rage Romulus slew his brother. When the city was built, on the seven hills which give it its other well-known name, it was named after Romulus.

But Romulus always bitterly regretted killing his brother and he always kept an empty throne beside him, as a symbol that Remus shared his power.

When he disappeared in the middle of a thunderstorm the citizens of Rome firmly believed that Romulus had been taken up in a fiery chariot to heaven by his father, the god Mars. Later they renamed Romulus Quirinus and worshipped him as a god.

In Kensington Gardens in London, near Long Water, there is a statue of Peter Pan, the boy who never grew up and who took the Darling boys and their sister Wendy to live with him and his boys so that Wendy could be a mother to all the children there.

Peter Pan was a character created by J. M. Barrie, and the statue, standing on a pedestal on which are carved fairies, rabbits and fieldmice, was erected in 1912. Among the other characters in the play are a pirate captain named Hook, an Indian princess called Tiger Lily and a fairy named Tinker Bell.

At Kamakura, near Tokyo in Japan, there is a giant statue of Buddha, cast in bronze with eyes of pure gold. It represents the Amitabha Buddha who his followers believe lives in Pure Lane Paradise, and all devout Buddhists offer prayers to this god. But the founder of Buddhism was the son of a rich maharajah who renounced a life of luxury to become a poor man. He cut his hair and became a monk and he sat under a tree contemplating his life. He preached his first sermon at the city of Benares, which later became a holy city to his followers.

Gautama became known as the Buddha, or 'The Enlightened One', because of the Four Noble Truths which he preached. These were that man could not escape suffering, suffering is caused by selfish desires, it can be cured by concern for others instead of oneself, and that all devout Buddhists must follow the 'Middle Way' to Nirvana.

FOOD FOR THOUGHT!

What did Persephone eat during her stay in the underworld?

Six pomegranate seeds, and as a result of this she had to stay in Hades for six months of the year as Queen. During this time her mother Ceres mourned the loss of her daughter and this was when winter came to the earth. But when Persephone returned above ground for her summer stay, corn grew and flowers bloomed until it was time for her to return to her husband once again.

Who is said to have burned the cakes?

Alfred, King of Wessex, was said to have let the cowherd's wife's cakes burn when she asked him to watch them in return for safe shelter after a weary battle with the Viking invaders in the Athelney marshes.

Not realising that her guest was the king himself, the peasant woman scolded the monarch soundly for spoiling the cakes, and an embarrassed King Alfred left the cottage without telling the woman who he was.

But the episode was later recounted to a monk named Father Neot who told the story in his *Chronicles of St. Neot's*, a history of that period. Without this we would never have learned about the king's carelessness.

Can you name the fruit which lost Atalanta a race?

An oracle warned Atalanta, daughter of the king of Boeotia, that marriage would bring her unhappiness. So when she was of marriageable age Atalanta said that she would only marry a man who could outrun her, for she was extremely fleet of foot.

Because of her great beauty many men took up her challenge, although they knew that the penalty for failure was death. Many young men died and Atalanta remained free until one day a youth named Hippomenes saw her and fell in love with her. But Hippomenes knew he needed something else beside the skill of his running to win the race. So he sought the help of the Goddess of Love, Aphrodite, whom others called Venus.

Aphrodite gave Hippomenes three beautiful golden apples, telling him to drop them in front of Atalanta during the race.

Hippomenes did as the goddess told him, dropping an apple at various intervals during the race. The last apple was the most beautiful of all, and Atalanta gazed at it for a few precious moments as she held it in her hand after picking it up . . . just long enough for Hippomenes to win the race.

But although she had lost the race, Atalanta prized the golden apples, and she was perfectly willing to marry the victor, for Hippomenes was both young and handsome.

But in his joy at winning Atalanta for his bride, Hippomenes forgot to offer thanks to Aphrodite for the part the goddess had played in his victory.

This made Aphrodite very angry and she made Cybele, the goddess of the earth, very angry with the lovers. As a result Cybele turned Atalanta and her husband into lions and forced them to pull her chariot for the rest of their lives.

And so, despite all Atalanta's precautions, her marriage did bring her disaster . . . as a result of stopping to pick up three golden apples.

Why does a jumping bean jump?

Because it contains the imprisoned larva of a moth which has laid an egg in the bean before the bean was fully formed. These very unusual beans come from Mexico.

WOULD YOU BELIEVE IT?

All the ideas on these two pages are thought by many people to be absolutely true. But are they? Let's find out if any of them really have any foundation in fact . . .

OSTRICHES HIDE THEIR HEADS IN THE SAND

No ostrich living in captivity or in the wild has ever been seen to do such a thing. At the approach of another animal they sometimes bend their necks close to the ground and listen intently, and this may be what has given rise to the belief. The ostrich in fact has a much better way of coping with possible attack from an enemy. It runs away.

BROWN EGGS ARE MORE NUTRITIOUS THAN WHITE

The colour of the shell has nothing whatever to do with the quality of an egg. Although to most of us a brown egg generally looks much more appetising than a white one, in some countries it is quite the opposite, and white eggs are thought to be somehow purer than brown. Again, not true!

CARROTS HELP YOU SEE IN THE DARK

One of the basic requirements for good vision in poor light is a diet which contains adequate amounts of Vitamin A, found in milk, butter and green vegetables. This vitamin assists in the formation of 'visual purple', which is a pigment in the retina. Carrots contain a substance called carotene, and this is converted by the body into Vitamin A. The belief that carrots help you see in the dark therefore, is founded on scientific fact – but it certainly isn't true that you will suddenly be able to see clearly in pitch blackness if you've just munched your way through a bunch of them!

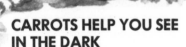

THE DEATH PENALTY HAS BEEN ABOLISHED IN BRITAIN

Capital punishment for crimes of murder has been abolished in Britain, but there are still two offences for which the penalty is death by hanging. The first is treason, which covers a number of exceptionally serious crimes, including conspiring to kill the king or queen. And the second, intriguingly, is piracy with violence, which is a section of the Piracy Act of 1837 – an act which has never been repealed. Until 1971, when the law was changed, arson in a naval dockyard was also punishable by death.

IT IS SAFE TO REMOVE A SPLINTER WITH A NEEDLE BUT NOT WITH A PIN

Many people believe that splinters can be safely removed by using a needle, but that a pin is much more likely to cause infection. The belief probably came about because pins and needles were originally made of different metals, and somehow the idea spread that the metal used for pins was dangerous. Nowadays we realise that it is not the metal, but the germs carried on the metal, which cause infections. Always sterilise any splinter-removing implement in boiling water before use, never use a rusty point, and use plenty of antiseptic on the cut after the offending particle is removed.

LIGHTNING NEVER STRIKES TWICE

Scientists have yet to unravel all the mysteries of the phenomenon of lightning, and there is much they still have to discover about its causes and its nature. One thing they do know, however, is that it is by no means unusual for it to strike in the same place twice. Lightning generally strikes prominent buildings, and when there are frequent storms in one area those buildings are likely to be struck repeatedly. The Empire State building, for instance, was struck 68 times during its first ten years.

RED SKY AT NIGHT, SHEPHERDS' DELIGHT

This belief, along with as many as half of the most familiar weather proverbs, has been found to be almost always true. It is well known in several countries of the world, and it is even mentioned in the Bible. The other part of the rhyme is 'Red sky at morning, shepherds' warning', and this too has proved itself to be a reliable 'barometer'. Test it out for yourself and see how many times the rhyme is proved to be accurate.

A LITTLE DUTCH BOY SAVED HOLLAND FROM FLOODING

The stirring tale is often told of the brave little Dutch boy who saved Holland from flooding by putting his finger in a hole in a dyke. Sadly, this charming story has no basis in fact, though it does exist quite definitely in fiction. The tale was invented by a nineteenth-century American writer, Mary Mapes Dodge, and it appeared in some editions of her book *Hans Brinker, or The Silver Skates*. The idea of the brave little boy sitting all night with his finger in the icy water of the dyke has so captivated succeeding generations of readers that it has now passed into the realms of popular folklore.

HOW MUCH DO YOU KNOW ABOUT THE HISTORY OF CLOTHES?

What were the first shoes like?

They were often knitted or sewn stockings; later these were made from animal skins and in bad weather covered by a simple wooden sandal. In the warmer countries, sandals with leather thongs were worn from the earliest times. There was little change in footwear until the seventeenth century when the first heeled shoes came into being, trimmed with lace and ribbons. From then on heels have remained important. Later leather boots were invented. In modern times shoes are made from wood, rubber, cloth and synthetics as well as from leather.

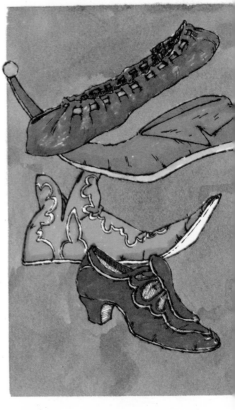

What was a doublet?

This was originally the padded coat worn beneath a breastplate. Later it became the main garment that a man wore beneath his heavy coat or cloak. From the fifteenth to the seventeenth centuries the doublet was affected by different fashions, and sometimes was very finely made of expensive cloth, slashed and puffed to make the wearer seem bigger. Henry VIII was fond of these bulky garments. By the seventeenth century the doublet grew smaller until its function was taken over by the waistcoat.

What was the 'hobble skirt'?

A long skirt which was so narrow around the ankles that walking normally was difficult – women tended to hobble instead. Fashionable between 1910 and 1914, it became popular because a famous actress used it on stage for an original role. Since she wore it only because the role required her to stand motionless against a pillar for some hours and wanted a dress to match the pillar's shape, it was a surprise to many when the hobble skirt's followers wore it to walk, dance and be generally active. But its impracticality ensured it was not fashionable for very long.

When was the umbrella first thought of?

After a kind of umbrella was used by the ancient peoples as a sunshade, it was not seen again until the sixteenth century when a giant umbrella was made for several people at once! Marie de Medici took the fashion to France, when sunshade umbrellas and parasols were made of waxed material with horn handles. But 'wet weather' umbrellas came into their own in the eighteenth century. Made of oiled cloth and cane, they were heavy and unfashionable, but they paved the way for lighter, more practical umbrellas which became an essential for every well-dressed man. For a while parasols with fancy fringing and silk covers were invaluable for shielding the sun from women; but now most people wear sunglasses instead.

Who created the 'New Look'?

The famous French fashion designer Christian Dior began a revolution in women's clothes when his 'New Look' came out in 1947. After the dreariness and skimpy line of the clothes worn throughout the Second World War his more feminine approach, of small waists and wide, full skirts, caught the world's imagination, and set the style for the fifties. It wasn't until the sixties, and the advent of the mini-skirt, that Dior's 'New Look' fell from the forefront of fashion.

What is the history of the handbag?

During the Middle Ages women tied purses to a belt around their waists. These were called aumonieres, after the French word for alms, and held coins and other small objects. Later there was a Gothic fashion entailing the wearing of many different bags around the waist! Later, ladies had small draw-string bags to hold, either sewn or knitted. This was the fore-runner of the Victorian reticule, a bag on a long cord. It wasn't until the last quarter of the nineteenth century that strong, stiff handbags became known, rather the same as the handbags in fashion today.

RED AS . . .

What is a mantella?

A mantella is a beautiful orange-red frog which lives in Madagascar.

Where is 'the rose-red city'?

The 'rose-red city, half as old as time', is Petra in Jordan, now in ruins. It can only be reached through narrow gorges of red sandstone cliffs, but when it was discovered in 1812, archaeologists discovered the remains of beautiful tombs and an amphitheatre.

Who were the 'Redbreasts'?

This was the nickname given to the Bow Street Runners, the forerunners of the new police force in the mid-nineteenth century. They wore a blue dress-coat with brass buttons and a bright red-cloth waistcoat, hence their nickname.

Who was Eric the Red?

Eric the Red's full name was Eric Thorwaldson, and he was a Norseman who explored Greenland and set up a colony there in the late tenth century. He was the first European to record a voyage on the Atlantic Ocean. His son Lief Ericson later visited Norway, the land from which Eric and his father had once fled, where Lief learned about Christianity which he in turn spread in his father's colony of Greenland.

Who founded the Red Cross?

Jean Henri Dunant, a Swiss banker and philanthropist, founded the Red Cross after seeing the suffering of the wounded during the mid-nineteenth century Austro-Sardinian War. 'The Committee of Five' met in Geneva and as a result the *Geneva Convention* was signed, for the protection and care of wounded soldiers in war. Later came the International Red Cross Committee, with branches in most countries of the world.

In both war and peace the Red Cross help the suffering with medical aid, food parcels, finding missing relatives and so on. There is also a Junior Red Cross which help the ill and handicapped, visit hospitals and shop for disabled people. The junior branch also run their own special projects such as an Austrian camp for diabetic children and a Greek school which is run entirely by funds supplied by a Canadian school.

The Red Cross Flag honours Switzerland where the Red Cross was founded in 1863. The Swiss flag is a white cross on a red background, so a red cross on a white field was chosen as the new name and emblem of this mercy mission. In non-Christian countries a red crescent is the emblem instead of a cross.

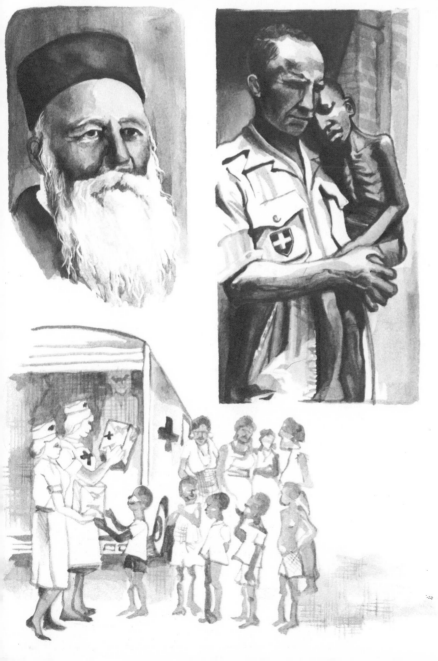

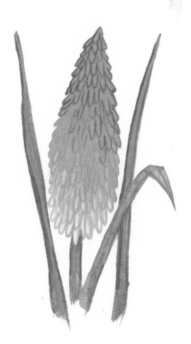

Where would you find a red-hot poker?

Growing in a garden, as it is a flower, a member of the lily family. It grows up to nine feet tall and its upright flower spikes remind one of a hot poker, hence its name, as the flowers change from glowing red, through orange to yellow.

It is also known as the Torch Flower and although coming originally from South Africa it can now be seen in many gardens during spring and early autumn.

THE WORLD OF EXPLORERS

Who was Marco Polo?

In 1271, young Marco Polo (1254-1324) set out with his father and uncle to journey from Italy to the legendary empire of *Cathay* (China) ruled by the mighty Kublai Khan. Marco travelled far and wide in the imperial service of the Khan and was keenly interested in everything he saw, the splendours of the East being, at that time, far in advance of Europe.

They returned home in 1295, laden with silks, jewels and wonderful tales of Cathay's wealth and vastness. Marco Polo's vivid, detailed descriptions inspired a whole new age of exploration.

Which ship first circumnavigated the world?

Ferdinand Magellan (1480-1521) left Spain in 1519 with five ships, to find the fabled westward route to the Indies. Three ships survived to round the tip of South America, then Magellan sailed 1,000 miles northwards along the coast, before striking west across the Pacific. For three desperate months the crews suffered near-starvation and disease before reaching hospitable land.

Shortly afterwards Magellan was killed. Further misfortunes followed, and in September 1522 only one ship, the **Victoria,** sailed into Seville after a journey of almost three years.

Who discovered the source of the White Nile?

The mystery of the source of the Nile fascinated geographers from the earliest times, but it was not until the 19th century that serious expeditions were mounted to discover it.

John Hanning Speke (1827-64) first discovered *Lake Victoria*, which he believed to be the source, in 1858, but his claim was disputed. A new expedition provided further proof in July 1862, and Samuel Baker and H.M.Stanley later confirmed his discoveries. As a reward, Speke was allowed the right to add a hippopotamus and a crocodile to his coat-of-arms.

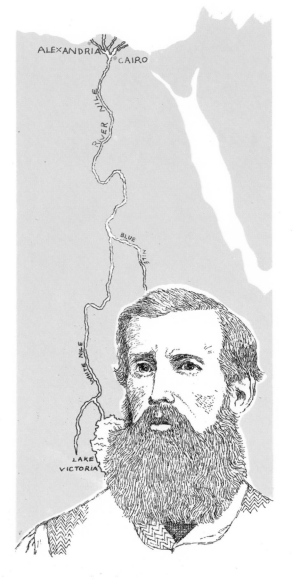

Who was the first Englishman to reach the South Pole?

Cap.Robert Falcon Scott reached the South Pole on 17th January 1912, a month after the Norwegian, Amundsen. Though bitterly disappointed, Scott's efforts contributed immeasurably to our scientific understanding of the Antarctic.

The ensuing Polar winter seriously deteriorated surface conditions; this, together with extremely severe weather, disastrously slowed their return. Scott's refusal to abandon two seriously ill men, Evans and Oates, further reduced their speed.

Desperate fuel shortages cut their hot food ration, and finally, only 11 miles from a supply depot, Scott and his surviving companions, Wilson and Bowers, perished, confined to their tent by a violent blizzard.

THE OLYMPICS

According to legend, Heracles, the patron of athletes, marked out the original Olympic stadium with 600 footsteps imprinted in the sand—an equivalent to a distance of 192.70 metres.

Who first said 'The most important thing is not to win, but to take part'?

These words were first spoken by the Archbishop of Philadelphia during a ceremony held in honour of the athletes for the 1908 Games, which were held in London. They were elaborated on in a speech by Baron de Coubertin later that year, and have often been used since as an expression of the spirit of the Olympics.

What is the Olympic motto?

It is the Latin *citius, altius, fortius,* which means 'faster, higher, stronger'. This motto is attributed to Father Didon, a friend of Pierre de Coubertin, who was responsible for the re-establishment of the Games in modern times.

When were the first modern Olympic Games?

They were held during April 1896 in Athens. Altogether 311 athletes competed, of whom 230 were Greek. The highlight was the marathon, run from Marathon to Athens, in which a humble water-carrier from Athens delighted the patriotic crowd by winning the gruelling three-hour race.

Who designed the Olympic flag, what is its emblem and when was it first displayed?

The flag was designed by none other than de Coubertin, and shows the five Olympic rings. De Coubertin himself described the flag as 'white, except for the five intertwined rings: blue, yellow, black, green and red. It symbolises the five land masses united by olympism and reproduces the colours of every nation'.

This latter was a reference to the world's flags, which are all covered by these six colours (including white), while the five land masses are our five continents.

The flag was first displayed at the Sorbonne in 1914, and has been used at all the Games since 1920.

In 1976 the Olympic flame was lit simultaneously in Olympia and in Montreal, using a laser beam.

What is the other famous Olympic symbol?

The flame. This was introduced by the Olympic Congress in 1925 (in honour of the ancient custom) and was first used in modern Olympics at the 1928 Amsterdam Games.

In 1936 the flame was lit for the first time at Olympia itself, using the original method of laying a piece of wood on a concave mirror and exposing it to sunlight until it caught fire. The flame was then carried to Berlin, the site of that year's Games, by a relay of runners, a practice which was to continue in the years to come.

HOW MUCH DO YOU KNOW . . .

ABOUT PLANTS?

On which side of a tree does moss grow?

Usually on the north side. This is because moss likes moist places and obviously there is least sunlight falling on the north side of a tree, making it darker and damper than the rest of the tree trunk.

Deep in a forest, however, where the rays of the sun cannot penetrate, moss may well grow on all sides of the trees.

How can you tell poison ivy from other plants?

By its leaves. There is a saying 'Leaflets three, let it be' which comes from the fact that poison ivy leaves are made up of three leaflets, two of which form a pair on opposite sides of a stem while the third lies by itself at the end of the stem.

Although the plant woodbine could in some ways easily be confused with poison ivy—which grows as either a bush or a vine, with shiny green leaves in the summer turning bright red in the autumn—the saying about the leaves still holds true, for woodbine clearly has five leaflets instead of the ivy's three.

Why isn't a mushroom green, like most plants?

Because it is a fungus. Fungi do not contain chlorophyll, which is what gives plants their green colour. Since chlorophyll is needed by plants to make their own food, mushrooms and other non-green plants have to absorb their food from elsewhere, for instance from the soil, which is rich with decaying plants.

Are there any animal-eating plants?

Yes, although they do not eat anything larger than insects (which, of course, are members of the animal kingdom).

These carnivorous plants capture their prey using various means. The *pitcher plant* has tubelike leaves that hold water, and insects crawl down into these leaves only to be caught on tiny hairs which line the tube. They then slide down the tube into the water, where eventually they drown.

The *sundew* has circular leaves, this time covered with hairs on the outside. Each hair has a drop of sticky liquid at its tip which holds onto the insect and prevents its escape, while the leaf curls inwards and traps it, ready for eating.

But perhaps the most well-known animal-eating plant is the aptly-named *Venus' fly-trap* This has hinged leaves, again with hairs over their surface. When an insect lands on one of these especially sensitive hairs, the leaf closes up on its hinge, trapping the insect inside.

WHO WAS THE MONA LISA?

Da Vinci's *Mona Lisa* is probably the world's masterpiece. It is the best-known and most priceless painting in the world. Leonardo took four years to complete it, while he was working on murals for the Palazzo Vecchio in Florence.

The woman he chose to paint was Lisa Gherardini, the sixteen-year-old who had become, in 1492, the third wife of an elderly Florentine nobleman called Francesco di Zanobi del Giocondo (hence the Mona Lisa's other name, La Gioconda). Giocondo didn't commission da Vinci to paint the portrait – unusual in a time when most works of art were commissioned. When it was completed da Vinci sold it to Francis I for 4,000 pieces of gold, and it has remained in France ever since, where it now hangs in the Louvre.

Perhaps the most famous feature of the painting is the smile. The *Mona Lisa*, if you look carefully, smiles with only the left part of her mouth. In fact it has been discovered, through the discovery of a book printed in 1541 called 'Concerning The Perfect Beauty of A Lady', that smiling in this way was a kind of fashion, thought to make a woman more alluring.

Lisa Gherardini was very beautiful in her own right, of course, despite the fashionable smile. Leonardo recalls in journals that he had lute music played and books read aloud while she sat for him, so that her lovely expression wouldn't fade through boredom.

Instead of dressing in opulent clothes and jewels for the portrait, as was the custom with noblewomen, Lisa was dressed simply and darkly. Her plain clothes add dramatic atmosphere and depth to the painting, blending with the sombre background of lonely countryside.

For many people the difference between a portrait and a masterpiece lies in the way that da Vinci had portrayed Lisa Gherardini's soul and character in a three-dimensional way. Leonardo made good use of his extensive knowledge of anatomy to create perfect figures, correct in every way, while his poetic insight enabled him to go deeper into the character of his sitter. In other words, he was able to reconcile scientific with imaginative exactness – a feat which troubles a great many artists.

It was this problem – of bringing to a flat canvas the world of secret thoughts and moods – which Leonardo struggled with all his life. He tried to create a visual equivalent for subjects which were intangible and invisible.

In the *Mona Lisa* are symbols of the hidden personality of a woman, set down by a genius. Da Vinci tried to portray many unspoken things which he saw in Lisa Gherardini's face. It is the power and truth of these unspoken things which we have recognised and admired through the centuries since the *Mona Lisa* was painted.

LITERARY NICKNAMES

Who was 'The Swan of Denmark'?

Hans Christian Andersen, born in Odense, the son of a poor shoe-maker, who was destined to become one of the world's greatest fairytale writers. He wanted to be an actor, but his efforts in this direction were mocked, so he turned to writing. Among his best known stories are *The Ugly Duckling* who like Andersen himself finally turned into a swan, *Thumbelina* and *The Little Mermaid*, a statue of which stands in Copenhagen harbour, a lasting remembrance to this wonderful teller of fairytales.

Who was 'Currer Bell'?

This was the pen name adopted by Charlotte Bronte when she first wrote her famous novel *Jane Eyre*, not wishing the publisher to know that she was a woman. Her two sisters, Anne and Emily wrote under the names of Ellis and Acton Bell. Charlotte was the eldest of these three daughters of Patrick Bronte, and was born in Yorkshire where she later lived at Haworth Parsonage with her father, her two older sisters, who sadly died in girlhood, and her brother Branwell. Charlotte also wrote *Villette* and *The Professor* which were based on her own experiences while teaching at a school in Brussels. Anne wrote *Tenant of Wildfell Hall* and Emily is remembered for her magnificent *Wuthering Heights*.

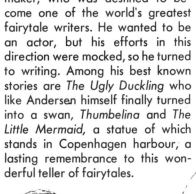

Who was 'George Eliot'?

This manly pen name hid the true name of the assistant editor of the Westminster Review, a young lady who was the daughter of a Warwickshire estate manager, Mary Ann Evans. Among her better known works are *Adam Bede*; *The Mill on the Floss*, in which the Tulliver family are drawn from Mary Ann's own family life; *Silas Marner*, the story of a miser and the foundling he took into his home; *Middlemarch* and *Daniel Deronda*.

Who was 'Boz'?

Sketches by Boz, a series of articles on London life, was one of the early works of Charles Dickens, who wrote them while working as a reporter in the House of Commons.

Dickens put much of his own life into his later novels, especially *David Copperfield* in which he recalled his days working in a bottle factory, where he put labels on bottles. He also wrote *The Old Curiosity Shop* at the end of which the whole nation wept at the death of Little Nell; *Nicholas Nickleby*, the adventures of a young schoolmaster in a very bad school in Yorkshire; *Bleak House*, and two of the most loved of all, *Pickwick Papers* which told of the amusing adventures of Samuel Pickwick and his friends, and in *A Christmas Carol*, the tender tale of Tiny Tim, who finally helped to melt the hard heart of Ebenezer Scrooge. Dickens gave public performances of his own work, both at home and in the United States. He died suddenly in 1870 at the age of 58.

HOW DOES IT WORK?

The Microwave Oven

The microwave oven has been heralded as a major breakthrough, first in the catering trade, and now in the domestic kitchen. But what exactly is a microwave oven, and how does it work?

The microwave is really a super-speedy oven that will cook food in an amazingly short time. For instance, it takes just fifteen minutes to cook a whole chicken! It will also cook frozen food without it having to be defrosted first.

How? It is all made possible by very high frequency radio waves, which penetrate the food to be cooked, violently agitating the molecules therein. This agitation creates great heat, so that the food cooks *internally*, rather than *externally*.

The source of the microwaves is a magnetron, a high-frequency radar tube. Microwaves generated by the magnetron travel down a metal duct, are reflected into the oven, and dispersed evenly. The waves are reflected around the oven until they are absorbed by the food.

What happens to the food? Take a chicken. The molecules in it have plus and minus electrical charges, lined up in all directions. When microwave energy passes through the food the molecules are all aligned parallel with their electromagnetic field. The next pulse of energy reverses them.

Pulsed oscillations occur billions of times *per second*, producing tremendous frictional heat. This accounts for the extra-fast cooking time, the food cooking from within. It is because of this internal cooking that joints of meat etc don't brown in a microwave, even when they are cooked through.

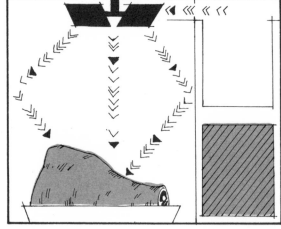

rotating reflector blades

microwaves are reflected until absorbed by the food

high voltage power supply

Microwave ovens are a potentially dangerous form of radiation. For this reason the ovens are metal-lined and have strong doors. The cooker will not function until the doors are closed, thus ensuring safety.

WHAT HAPPENS IN A MICROWAVE OVEN

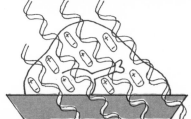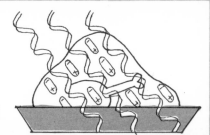

1. The molecules in a chicken have plus and minus electrical charges oriented every way.

2. A pulse of microwave energy passing through the chicken aligns the molecules parallel with their electromagnetic field.

3. The next pulse reverses them. Pulsed oscillations occur billions of times per second, producing frictional heat and cooking the chicken very quickly from within.

QUESTIONS AND ANSWERS

What was the Gordian Knot?

The Gordian Knot was, in Greek mythology, a knot tied so intricately that no one could untie it. It was first tied by a peasant called Gordius to tie the ox yoke to his chariot. Later, Gordius was made a King because the oracle advised it, and Gordius dedicated his chariot and yoke to Zeus. A legend grew up that the man who could loosen the knot would rule all Asia, and later Alexander the Great cut the knot through with his sword to fulfil the prophecy. Researchers in recent times have found a tomb thought to belong to King Gordius. The term 'cutting the Gordian Knot' means tackling a difficult problem in a clever way.

What are gargoyles?

Gargoyles are decorated water-spouts jutting out from the gutters of roofs. The word gargoyle comes from the Latin gurgulio, meaning gullet. Greek and Roman architects placed open-mouthed lions at the edges of each roof, so that water sliding down would empty from their mouths. Gargoyles became a favourite feature of Gothic architects, used in the building of churches, cathedrals and other buildings. They were weird half-human, half-animal creatures. Keeping an eye out for them is a fascinating pastime.

Who was Muhammed?

Muhammed was a prophet who lived in the early A.D. 600s. He preached in Mecca that there was only one god, Allah, and that he, Muhammed, was the messenger of Allah. People who follow Muhammed's religion are called Muslims, meaning 'one who submits to God'. The religion is called Islam, Arabic for submission. Islam has more than 400 million followers, most of whom live in or around the Middle East, North Africa and Indonesia and the Philippines in the East.

The rapid spread of Islam resulted in the Crusades being fought between Christians and Muslims. The Holy Book of Islam is called the Koran, made up from Muhammed's teachings.

What language is spoken in India?

In fact Indians speak about sixty different languages, with fourteen major ones. The two main families to which each language belongs are the Dravidian and the Indo-European. The Indo-European languages are spoken in northern India and include Hindi and Urdu, which includes many Persian words. Hindi is more influenced by Sanskrit, an ancient Indian language related to Greek and Latin. A simpler form of Hindi and Urdu is Hindustani.

The main Dravidian languages are Kanada, Tamil and Telugu. They are spoken mainly in the south. Nearly half the people can speak Hindi, which is the official language. English remains as an 'associate official language'.

सत्यमेव जयते

What is a hybrid?

A hybrid is the offspring of two plants or animals of different genetics. The young of a donkey and a mare is a mule; the grapefruit and the tangerine bred together produce the ugli fruit. The orange and the tangerine became the ortanique, and the buffalo and domestic cow becomes a cattabu. Hybridisation is important because breeders can produce variations which are more suitable for what is wanted than would be possible otherwise.

DO YOU KNOW?

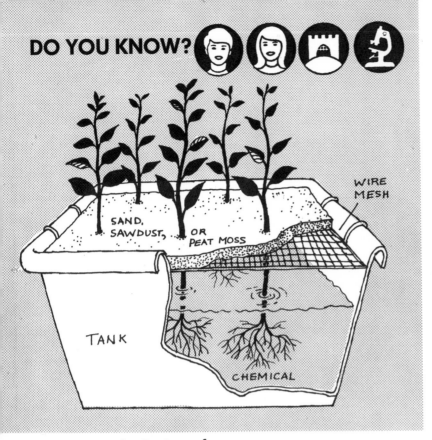

What is hydroponics?

A method of growing plants without soil. Plants are supplied with water which has been reinforced with various mineral salts to help good growth. The seeds are planted in a layer of damp sawdust, sand or moss and grow through this, and through a wire mesh, until the roots are taking nourishment from the water. Plants grown this way tend to be sturdier since they are not vulnerable to infections and insects in ordinary soil.

Why are the Society of Friends called Quakers?

George Fox founded the Society of Friends, a religious sect, in 1648. His followers were first called Quakers after Fox told a judge to "tremble at the word of the Lord".

Which woman won the Nobel Prize?

A British chemist, Dorothy Crowfoot Hodgkin, was awarded the Nobel Prize in 1964 for her work in chemistry. She found the structures of substances such as penicillin and vitamin B12. She went to Oxford and received the Order of Merit in 1965.

HOW DID JIGSAWS COME INTO BEING?

In the London of the 1760s lived and worked a young man called John Spilsbury, an engraver and map-maker. One day he had an idea for a learning aid for children that was revolutionary, especially in those days, with books specially written for children only having appeared a few years before.

John pasted maps onto blocks of wood, cut the blocks into separate pieces, and put the pieces into special polished wood boxes. The child had to fit the pieces of wood together, thus completing the map and improving his geographical knowledge.

At that time children were expected to learn from a very early age, and had few of the pleasures of childhood as we know it today. Latin and Greek were usual subjects for five-year-olds, and poor children were expected to go out to work and earn a living at the age of seven. You can imagine how well the 'dissected maps' were received by hard-worked young scholars, for they provided a little entertainment amid hours of study, though they were expensive, and therefore only available to rich children.

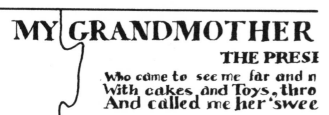

MY GRANDMOTHER

THE PRESI

Who came to see me far and n
With cakes and Toys, thro
And called me her 'swee

HER!   M>

Who bade me duly kee
To be to ev'ry creatu
And look with pity on

HER!   M

SICKNESS

Who when the smallpo
All sad hung o'er her l
And wept for joy whe

HER!   M

John Spilsbury's idea soon spread to Europe and America, and many new ideas appeared on what came to be called 'dissected puzzles' – dates, lists of kings and queens, the alphabet, multiplication tables etc. In fact their popularity increased so much that they were eventually used as toys purely and simply, featuring scenes, verses and rhymes.

As methods of making the puzzles increased, wood gave way to cardboard, and now jigsaws are enjoyed by people of all ages, and range from simple pre-school standard of about eight pieces to complicated scenes made up from many thousands of pieces.

But what of their modern name? John Spilsbury's 'dissected maps' and 'dissected puzzles' were popular for many years, the name jigsaw not being used in Britain until this century. The word probably originated in America, where the saw used to cut the puzzles is known as a jigsaw.

BOOKWORMS QUIZ

Just how much do you think you know about the world of literature? Test yourself with this quiz!

1. Do you know which famous author travelled all over Britain for his job with the Post Office, and still had time to write fifty books?

2. What was the name of the island Gulliver discovered at the beginning of his travels?

3. Alexander Selkirk was a Scots sailor who, after an argument with his captain, was left behind on a deserted island. Later Daniel Defoe wrote a book based on Selkirk's experiences. Do you know its name?

4. An ill-educated tinker's son went on to write a masterpiece about a character called Christian. Can you name the author and his book?

5. This Victorian author's pen-name was, for a while, 'Boz'. Who was he really?

6. Peter Pan lived, in J.M. Barrie's book, in a special kind of land. What was it called?

7. Do you know which book featured Mole, Toad and Ratty? And, if so, can you name its author, too?

8. Anna Sewell wrote a story about a magnificent animal. What animal was it, and what was its name?

9. Can you name the three female novelists who once lived together in Haworth Parsonage?

10. The Brothers Grimm wrote and collected German fairytales. But do you know what their careers were?

11. Have you ever read any of P.C. Wren's adventure stories about the Foreign Legion? Give the name of his most famous novel.

12. *First Impressions* was the original title of Jane Austen's first book. By what name would we know the novel today?

15. A Scots poet and author wrote about the heroes Rob Roy and Ivanhoe. Do you know who he was?

16. The "Just-So" stories are well-loved all over the world. But who wrote them?

13. Someone tilted at windmills and rode a mount called Rozinante, in Cervantes' great book. Who was he—and do you know the name of his fat companion, too?

14. James Fenimore Cooper was a writer who concentrated on portraying a certain race of people. Who were these people?

17. Edgar Rice Burroughs invented a legend with his books. Do you know what character he created?

18. A modern American author wrote a lovely story about the biggest pearl in the world. He was born in California and lived there most of his life. Who was he?

19. *Elidor* and *The Weirdstone of Brisingamen* are only two of the magical books written by—who?

20. Kate Greenaway was famous for her skill with books. But what exactly was she?

ANSWERS

11. *Beau Geste*
12. *Pride and Prejudice*.
13. Don Quixote—and Sancho Panza.
14. American Indians.
15. Sir Walter Scott.
16. Rudyard Kipling.
17. Tarzan.
18. John Steinbeck.
19. Alan Garner.
20. She was an illustrator.

1. Anthony Trollope.
2. The island of Lilliput.
3. *Robinson Crusoe*.
4. John Bunyan; *The Pilgrim's Progress*.
5. Charles Dickens.
6. Never-never Land.
7. Kenneth Grahame; *Wind In The Willows*.
8. A horse; the book *Black Beauty*.
9. Anne, Emily and Charlotte Brontë.
10. Professors.

RUSSIA

Empire of Two Continents

Russia – or the U.S.S.R., to use its proper name – is the largest country in the world, stretching from the Arctic in the North to the Pacific in the South. Some people prefer to call it an empire, which might be more appropriate. Although the official language is Russian, the people also speak over sixty other languages, and belong to national groups like the Georgians, the Tartars, the Uzbecks, the Kazakhs and the Armenians. In fact, only sixty per cent of the population are Russian!

Moscow, Russia's capital, is in Europe, and one of the largest cities in the world. Although about three-quarters of the country is in Asia, most of the important cities are in Europe: Leningrad, Minsk, Kiev and Gorki, to name but a few. Moscow in particular is a very beautiful city with many magnificent reminders of the days when the Tzars ruled Russia. The Peterhof and Winter Palaces, which are in Leningrad, used to be owned by the Russian royal family before the Revolution in 1917, when soviets (systems of councils) were set up to govern, giving Russia the name Soviet Union. Every year there is a May Day parade in the streets to commemorate the anniversary of the revolution.

The U.S.S.R. is a very beautiful land, but as you might expect, being so large it is also very varied. In the south you will find hot desert, while in Siberia, in the north, you'll discover the coldest climate in the world!

Lake Baykal, on the edge of the Central Siberian plateau, is the largest freshwater lake in Asia, and also has the deepest body of water – 1,700 metres deep! The Caspian sea, on the other hand, is the largest inland body of water in the world. It's called a sea because the water is salty.

There are many schools and universities in Russia, and a lot of industry as well as agriculture. In the East, communications are much more efficient than in the West of the country, but throughout the land the people rely mostly on railways, since the roads are poor. The Trans-Siberian railway goes from the centre of Moscow to the Pacific coast, and is 8,000 kms long! Main seaports are Odessa and Murmansk.

Russians use roubles as their financial system; 100 kopecks make one rouble. The State owns most of the businesses and stores in Russia, and they have a great many important museums and libraries. Everyone has heard of the Bolshoi Ballet and the Leningrad Kirov,

whose dancers tour the world with great success every year. Russia is famous for its love of the dance. Other achievements have been in space: Russia launched her space programme in 1961 and since then has sent the first woman into space, and the first man to float outside his craft.

In the U.S.S.R., women play an important part in the work of the country, by digging roads, working on construction sites and doing other jobs which are still

not deemed suitable for women in other countries.

Russia has thousands of newspapers, but the best known are *Pravda* (Truth); *Izvestia* (News) and *Red Star*. Quite a few people own television sets and radios, but there are relatively few private telephones. Loudspeakers broadcast programmes in parks and street corners for people to listen to freely.

Russia has a great cultural history. Tolstoy, Chekhov, Turgenev and Dostoyevsky all found literary success with their magnificent novels and plays in the nineteenth century, while musicians like Rimsky-Korsakov, Mussorgsky and Rachmaninoff created their expressive compositions from ancient folk tunes.

To many of us, Russia is a mysterious land, an unknown world, but as time passes more visitors go there to discover what lies behind the frontier of the world's largest country – an empire reaching over two continents, a land of snow and desert sun.

FAMOUS INVENTORS – OF WHAT?

1.

Sir Isaac Newton was the greatest mathematician of his time – perhaps of all time. His genius established laws and theorems that still hold true today, and one of them suggested itself to him as he watched an apple fall to the ground. Was it:

a) The displacement principal;

b) The law of gravity;

c) The theory of relativity.

3.

Michael Faraday was a protégé of the great chemist, Sir Humphrey Davy, but although the two scientists worked together initially, Faraday's research far outshone that of Davy. He discovered a way to harness something we now take for granted. Was it:

a) Electricity;

b) Steam;

c) Water.

4.

Guglielmo Marconi was an Italian inventor who came to England to complete his research. He won the Nobel Prize for physics, and his invention changed the pattern of communication all over the world. Was it:

a) The telegraph;

b) The wireless;

c) Morse code.

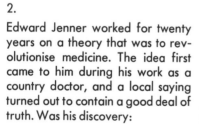

2.

Edward Jenner worked for twenty years on a theory that was to revolutionise medicine. The idea first came to him during his work as a country doctor, and a local saying turned out to contain a good deal of truth. Was his discovery:

a) Antiseptic;

b) Pasteurisation;

c) Vaccination.

Check your answers on page 191

What is the Book of Kells?

An illuminated manuscript of the Gospels by monks on Iona in the ninth century. The monks, driven from their monastery by a Viking attack, settled later in Kells, in Ireland. The book has some of the finest illuminated artwork in existence. It is kept in Trinity College in Dublin.

Who was the first man to reach the North Pole?

Robert Edwin Peary, on April 6th 1909. For a while argument raged between Peary and a Dr. Frederick Cook. Cook claimed he had reached the North Pole a year before, and his story reached the newspapers first. Peary was disbelieved, and robbed of the acclaim he deserved until the University of Copenhagen discredited Doctor Cook.

Who were the Fauves?

They were a group of young painters, Matisse, Derain and Rouault among them, who pioneered a new way of painting. They used realistic subjects but painted them in an unrealistic way, using aggressively bright colours. The point was to stimulate and shock, and this they did. At their first exhibition in 1905 a critic called them 'les fauves' (wild beasts), and the name stuck.

Who was Keir Hardie?

A miner who was born to poverty in Lanarkshire, Keir Hardie became the first working-class politician. A Liberal at the beginning of his career, he joined the Labour party which was then in its infancy and became the first Independent Labour Member of Parliament. As his influence grew he became a decisive force in British politics, and the Welfare State can in the main be attributed to him.

A LITERARY LINE-UP

Who created Sherlock Holmes?

Fiction's most famous detective was created by Sir Arthur Conan Doyle. Born in Edinburgh in 1859 he decided to become a doctor, and it was when he was studying medicine at unversity that he met the man who was to later inspire him to create his most famous character. The man was his professor, Joseph Bell, who was particularly good at finding out not only what ailed his patients but, through careful observation, details of their character, job and circumstances. It was his powers of 'deduction' that so impressed Conan Doyle and inspired him to create his famous detective.

In 1887 Conan Doyle published his first Sherlock Holmes book, *A Study in Scarlet*, featuring the super-sleuth and his friend Dr Watson, and in the years that followed many other books and short stories appeared, all eagerly awaited by Holmes' growing army of devotees. In fact, Conan Doyle somewhat resented the popularity of the Holmes stories, for he believed that his other work was equally as good, though not nearly so popular with the public. He tried to kill off Holmes in one story, but there was such an uproar that he was forced to bring the detective back for more adventures.

Although a successful writer, Conan Doyle continued to practise medicine, going to South Africa during the Boer War to treat injured troops, and he did some real-life sleuthing, too, championing those he believed had been wrongly convicted or badly treated. He was knighted in 1902.

Incidentally, the phrase that has come to be associated with Holmes—"Elementary, my dear Watson!"—does not appear in Conan Doyle's work!

Who wrote Dr Jekyll and Mr Hyde?

Edinburgh-born Robert Louis Balfour Stevenson (1850-1894) wrote that famous book, plus many other stirring adventures like *Kidnapped* and *Treasure Island*, rightly regarded today as classics.

Trained as a lawyer, he soon abandoned his studies for literature, and his first book, *An Inland Voyage*, appeared in 1878. Many others followed, and he soon became one of the best-loved authors of his time.

Ill-health forced him to leave Britain for a better climate, and he made his home on the island of Upolu, Western Samoa, where he died.

Who was Mark Twain?

Mark Twain was the pen name chosen by Samuel Langhorne Clemens, author of favourites like *The Adventures of Tom Sawyer*, *The Adventures of Huckleberry Finn*, *Life on the Mississippi* and *The Prince and the Pauper*.

After working as a printer and a Mississippi pilot, he turned to writing, telling with charm and humour of the American people and places he knew best, and creating, in Tom Sawyer and Huckleberry Finn, two of the best-loved young rogues in literature. He died in 1910, aged 75.

Mark Twain took his pen name from the Mississippi river pilots' jargon: 'by the mark twain', meaning two fathoms depth by the sounding line.

Who created the famous fictional detective, Hercule Poirot?

The popular Belgian detective features in many of the novels of Agatha Christie. Her first book, *The Mysterious Affair at Styles*, published when she was in her twenties, was the first of more than fifty detective novels she was to write, *The Murder of Roger Ackroyd* being considered one of the finest detective stories of all time.

Many of her novels were made into films, and one of her plays, *The Mousetrap*, has been running in London since 1952!

Who wrote The Wind in the Willows?

It was whilst he was still working as a Bank of England official that Kenneth Grahame published his first work, and it was when he was fifty-nine years old that his masterpiece appeared. He originally wrote *The Wind in the Willows*, a charming animal fantasy, for his young son, but it soon became a best-seller, and has remained so to this day.

RED LETTER DAYS

In olden times, days which were special appeared in red on the calendar — hence the expression 'Red Letter Day' meaning a day with a very special significance.

When is Mardi Gras?

Mardi Gras is the day before Lent begins, Shrove Tuesday, or as the words 'Mardi Gras' mean literally 'Fat Tuesday'.

Mardi Gras is celebrated in many countries of the world with gay colourful carnivals with people dancing and singing in the streets, using this day as the last time for frivolities before the serious season of Lent, which starts on Ash Wednesday, the next day.

In Nice there is a special monarch known as 'King Carnival' while a similar king presides over the many colourful carnival floats in New Orleans and Haiti.

The name is believed to have been used originally because at one time a fat, roasted ox was paraded through the streets of Paris on Shrove Tuesday, and housewives used up their flour and eggs by making pancakes since families were expected to eat very frugally throughout Lent.

Where and when would you see St. Nicholas and Black Peter?

St. Nicholas and his servant Black Peter can be seen in the streets of the Netherlands, Belgium and Luxembourg on December 6th, when the saint who gave his name to Santa Claus promises to return during the night to reward all good children with gifts. They, in turn, leave clogs filled with biscuits and sweets for the saint and his servant, but if the children have been naughty, they find the clogs filled with ashes the following morning.

Where is the festival of Ganesh celebrated?

Ganesh is the Indian god of good fortune, and festivals in his honour take place among the Hindus of Poona, Bombay and Madras. Clay models of the deity with the head of an elephant are taken through the streets to the sound of cymbals and drums before finally being immersed in the sea or a lake.

What is Teng Kao?

This is the 'Feast of High Flight' in China when young and old go to fly their kites. It is celebrated on the ninth day of the ninth month of the Chinese calendar, and as well as giving pleasure it also has a more serious purpose, as the Chinese believe that any bad deeds which the kiteflyer has done during the year will be taken away by the kite when it is cut loose. So, at the end of the day, the kites are allowed to fly away, and the kiteflyers go home with clear consciences once again . . . until next year.

Why do they celebrate Thanksgiving Day in the USA?

To recall the day in 1621 when the Pilgrim Fathers who had come over from England in the *Mayflower* gave thanks to God for having gathered in safely the lean harvest which was to last them throughout the winter.

Today Thanksgiving Day is celebrated on the fourth Thursday in November in most States and families enjoy such traditional food as turkey and pumpkin pie.

WOULD YOU BELIEVE IT?

There is a small shrew in Africa called the hero shrew, which although only a few inches long, is so hardy that a twelve-stone man could stand on it, and it would still be able to get up and scurry away, quite unharmed.

The horned toad, a North American species, has a strange method of defence. It squirts blood at its attacker from out of its eyes.

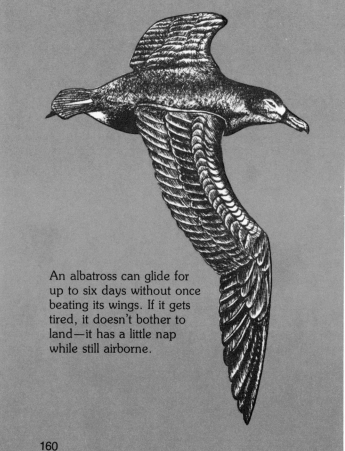

An albatross can glide for up to six days without once beating its wings. If it gets tired, it doesn't bother to land—it has a little nap while still airborne.

A snail can have as many as 25,000 teeth!

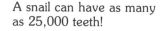

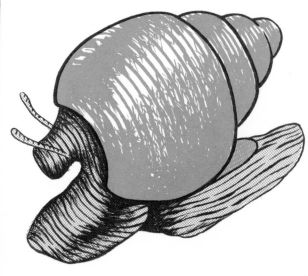

FAMOUS WOMEN – WHO WERE THEY?

1

This British nurse ran a Red Cross hospital for wounded troops in Belgium during the First World War. Although the Germans occupied the country, she was allowed to continue her work, and whenever she could she helped her patients to escape across the border to Holland. Finally she was arrested by the Germans and tried for treason. She was shot, in spite of appeals from the U.S.A. and other neutral countries, and her statue now stands opposite the National Portrait Gallery in London.
Who was she?

2

This Polish woman became the most famous of all women scientists. Determined, hard-working and a brilliant mathematician, she worked with her husband on the theory that radium was present in pitchblende. For four years she worked in an old shed, refining the tons of pitchblende until finally she obtained one-tenth of a grain of radio-active radium. She and her husband were awarded the Nobel Prize for their work in 1903, and she herself received a second Nobel Prize in Chemistry eight years later.
Who was she?

3

This American woman was a pioneer of modern dance in the early years of this century. She modelled her style of dancing on classical Greek art, and amazed her audiences by dancing barefoot, clad in scanty Greek tunics and floating scarves. She had many revolutionary ideas, including the use of music not written specially for dancing, and her free, expressive style greatly influenced modern dance. She opened dance schools in London, Paris, Berlin and Moscow.
Who was she?

4

This French woman was hailed as the greatest actress of her time. Her voice was legendary, and it was said that she could move an audience to tears by simply reciting the alphabet. She excelled in classical and romantic tragedy roles, and one of her most popular plays was *La Dame aux Camelias*. As well as acting, she managed several Paris theatres, and although she had her leg amputated in 1915 she did not retire from the stage until just before her death.
Who was she?

Check your answers on page 191

ALL ABOUT NICKNAMES

WHO WAS KNOWN AS 'EST-IL POSSIBLE'?

Prince George of Denmark, consort of Queen Anne, because he made this remark whenever a statement was made to him which he did not think could possibly be true . . . the first one being that his father-in-law James II had fled to France leaving the throne of England empty!

WHO OR WHAT IS 'AULD REEKIE'?

This is the name given to the old part of the city of Edinburgh because people often said that it was covered in a cloud of 'reek' or smoke.

WHO OR WHAT IS 'A FAIR MAID OF FEBRUARY'?

This is a country name for a snowdrop because these flowers usually appeared in early February. It was considered lucky to wish and touch the first snowdrop that was seen each year.

WHO WAS 'BUFFALO BILL'?

William Frederick Cody who was so called by the railroad men for whom he provided buffalo meat as food while they worked on the Kansas Pacific Railway. Later Bill headed a Wild West Show which appeared before the crowned heads of Europe as well as in all the major American cities.

FUN FACTS

SLOW COACHES

Tests on a giant tortoise show that its maximum speed on land is 0.17 m.p.h. A hungry tortoise enticed by a cabbage was unable to move more than five yards in a minute. Three-toed sloths are even slower. A female, goaded by the cries of her baby, reached a maximum 0.155 m.p.h. – nearly twice the usual speed.

NOT SO HARD CASH

Frenchman Francois Viete (1540–1603) could not sleep unless his pillow was resting on his entire personal fortune of £10,000.

SHORT TIME

If the existence of the Earth was reduced on a time scale to one year, humans would have made their first appearance on the 31st of December at 8.35 p.m. On the same scale, the Earth will be unable to support life – the sun will be too hot – in two years.

INDIAN TRAIL

Walking 'Indian file' comes from the practice of North American Indians, who, when walking through a forest, walked in the exact footprints of the man ahead so that the enemy could not tell how many of them there were.

STICK WITH IT

Novelist John Creasey of Bodenham received 743 rejection slips before his first book was accepted. Since then he has had 549 novels published under 25 different names.

EAT UP . . . OR ELSE!

The popularity of fish plummetted in England after the break with the Catholic Church allowed people to eat what they liked on Fridays. Frantic lobbying by the nation's fishermen persuaded Parliament not only to reinstate the custom, but to make failure to observe it punishable by law.

TOP THAT!

Robert Wadlow was still growing when he died in Michigan in 1940 at the age of 24 years 4 months. He measured 8 feet 11 inches and his hands were 12½ inches from the wrist to the tip of the middle finger.

ALL ABOUT FLOWERS

Do flowers grow in the desert?

Yes they do, although they grow only after rain, and flower for a short time before the sun dries them up. Desert annuals survive for most of the year as seeds, and their blooms are very brightly coloured to attract insects for pollination. The flowering Cactus plants store water in their thick fleshy stems, and their flowers are also very colourful.

Which is the largest flower in the world?

The largest flower in the world is the Giant Rafflesia, which grows in Malaysia and Indonesia. The flower itself may be up to three feet across, with petals up to one and a half feet long and an inch thick. The flower weighs between fifteen and twenty pounds.

What is an annual?

The term annual usually refers to a plant that only lives for one year, but some gardeners also use it to describe any plant that blooms within a year of the seeds being sown, no matter how long it lives after that. Common annuals are marigolds, cornflowers and groundsel.

Do all flowers grow from seeds?

No, some flowers reproduce without fertilization; like the crocus and daffodil, which grow from bulbs, or the strawberry, which sends out runners along the ground, each with a new plant on it.

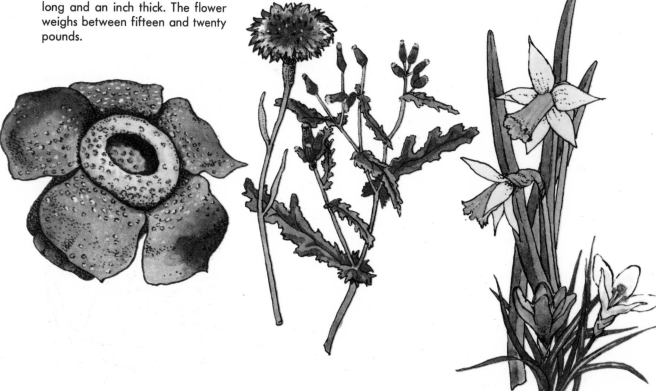

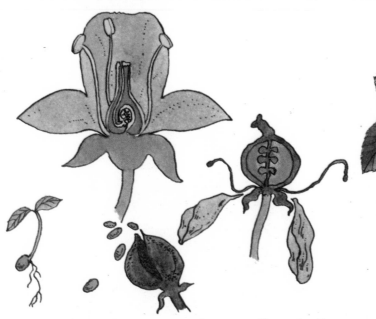

Why were red and white roses so significant in the fifteenth century?

They represented the two families fighting for the English throne. The white rose was the symbol of the followers of the Duke of York, and the red rose was the symbol of the House of Lancaster. The 'Wars of the Roses' as they were called, did not end until 1455, when the Yorkists won.

What is a perennial?

The term perennial refers to plants which live for several years or, in the case of roses, indefinitely. Most wild flowers are perennial, including daisies, buttercups, primroses and violets. Bulbs are perennial too.

What is pollination?

Pollination is the first step in the reproduction of flowers, and the process begins when the pollen is transferred from the stamens to the stigma. At the base of the stigma is the ovary, or egg cell, and once the pollen reaches this, fertilization takes place. This means that the ovary can now grow into a fruit with seeds, and it is from these seeds that a new flower will grow.

What are carnivorous plants?

These are plants which trap insects and small animals. They are found all over the world, and use various methods to trap their victims. The Pitcher plant has large, hollow leaves resembling a pitcher, and each is partly filled with sweet sticky liquid. The insects are attracted to this liquid, and once inside they drown. Butterworts have broad, sticky leaves on which insects get caught, while the Venus's fly-trap has leaves which snap shut when an insect crawls on the surface. In each case, the plant absorbs the liquid nourishment from the bodies of the decomposing insects.

THE WORLD ABOUT US

Where would you find the Ibo, the Fulani, the Yoruba and the Hausa?

In Nigeria, they are all native tribes. The Ibo live in the south east, the Fulani in the north, the Yoruba in the south west and the Hausa in the north. Each of these four tribes speaks its own language and the Hausa and the Fulani are excellent horsemen.

Who was Alfred Bernhard Nobel?

He was a Swedish chemist who invented dynamite and he also founded the Nobel Prizes. These are presented in Stockholm and Oslo each year under five separate categories to people who have worked for the good of humanity in their chosen fields. The five prizes are for work in physics, chemistry, physiology or medicine, literature and world peace.

What is Scotland Yard?

Scotland Yard is the headquarters of the London Metropolitan Police and it is to Scotland Yard that other police forces go for help and advice. Evidence is documented there of all crime and criminals, including records of fingerprints and information on the way certain criminals carry out their crimes.

The Aborigines of Australia use a certain tree to weave nets. What is this tree called?

The bottle tree. It has long narrow leaves, small clusters of flowers on slender stems and six seeds in each of its pod-shaped fruits.

What is the Morse Code?

A system devised by Samuel Morse whereby messages are sent by telegraph in a series of dots and dashes, a dash being equal to three dots in length. The dot is made by pressing and quickly releasing the key of the telegraph sending device.

Where is the Lorelei rock?

This will be found on the Rhine in Germany where legend says that the beautiful Lorelei maiden with golden hair sings so prettily that ships are lured onto the dangerous rocks, where they sink.

Who lived at Haworth Parsonage in Yorkshire, England?

The Brontë sisters, Anne, Emily and Charlotte with their widowed father and their brother Branwell. They wrote such classics as *Wuthering Heights*, *Jane Eyre* and *Tenant of Wildfell Hall* but, sadly, they all died at an early age.

What is bronze?

An alloy of copper and tin, which may contain a quarter of the total amount in tin. It is known for its hardness and durability and articles in bronze have been found which date back to 3,000 BC. Many Chinese ornaments are made in bronze, as it is a favourite material with many craftsmen.

DO YOU KNOW WHY?

WHY DO BIRDS BUILD THEIR NESTS HIGH IN TREES?

Not all birds build their nests high in trees, but many do, and there is a very good reason for it. When the young birds hatch from their eggs, they cannot fly, and they are very vulnerable. There is great danger from cats, foxes, weasels and other animals which prey on birds. High up in a tree, the young are much safer from all these threats. All birds do every–thing they can to ensure the safety of their young, and those which do not build their nests high in trees take various other precautions. Many ducks – mallards, for instance – build nests which are so well hidden that it is very difficult for predators to find them, and some sea birds nest high up on cliff ledges, which are completely inaccessible to most animal enemies.

WHY AREN'T ALL BIRDS' BEAKS THE SAME SHAPE?

The shape of a bird's beak – or bill, as it should really be called – depends on what kind of food the bird usually eats. Feeding habits differ a great deal, and while there are one or two species which will eat practically anything which is available, most birds stick to one particular kind of food. Let's look at three examples of birds with highly specialised bills. The woodcock has a long, thin bill, which is perfect for digging in soft ground to extract the worms which are its favourite food. The wide bill of the spoonbill gave this bird its name. It is just right for scooping up and filtering a wide variety of water plants, small fish, and water insects, in the shallow waters where it always feeds. Finches are always seed-eaters, and all species of finches have hard, conical beaks. Each species is slightly different though, and the hawfinch has a bill which is so strong that it can crack a cherry stone.

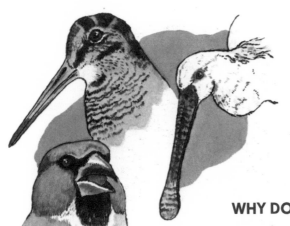

WHY DO OWLS ONLY HOOT AT NIGHT?

Owls are night birds, which means that they sleep through the day, and wake up when darkness falls. During the day, an owl can hardly see at all, because the bright light hurts its large eyes. At night though, it can see very clearly, and it becomes very active, hunting its prey of small animals and birds. When you listen to an owl's cries in the stillness of a dark night it's easy to see why many people have found the sound strange and eerie, echoing through the darkness. But it is also a lovely sound, and many people love to listen to it, as they lie in their beds.

WHY ARE MALE BIRDS OFTEN MORE BRIGHTLY COLOURED THAN FEMALES?

In the bird world, just as in all the animal worlds, it is very important for the adults of the species to find mates, to breed and to produce young. If this did not happen the entire species would die out. Thus the instinct to find a mate is very strong. The bright and attractive colouring of many male birds is intended to attract a female bird, and the male will spend a lot of time preening his feathers, to make sure that he is looking his best when the time for courtship comes near. One bird in particular has a really spectacular plumage, which it uses in its courtship displays. This bird is the peacock, and its partner, the pea-hen, looks drab indeed alongside her handsome mate. In some species of birds – robins, for instance – the two sexes are exactly alike in their plumage, and in these species other methods of choosing a mate have evolved.

WHY DON'T DUCKS FEEL COLD IN ICY WATER?

Ducks have a wonderful coat of feathers, which is specially designed to keep them warm and snug in even the coldest weather. First of all, they have an undercoat of soft downy feathers, which grow very close together, and trap a 'cushion' of air next to the duck's body. This stops the natural warmth of their bodies escaping into the cold outside. As for their top feathers, they protect these with a special oil which is secreted from a gland in their bodies. When you watch a duck preening its feathers, it is spreading this oil all over them, making its top coat of feathers completely waterproof. Neither water nor cold can penetrate the feathers from the outside, and the body warmth cannot escape through the down, and so the lucky duck stays warm and dry. Would you like a coat of feathers like that?

WHY DO DUCKS HAVE WEBBED FEET?

Ducks are water birds, and it is very important for them to be able to swim well. Their 'fingers' are joined by pieces of strong skin called webs, and these make the total area of each foot much larger. Their feet become like strong paddles. Using these 'paddles' they can swim swiftly through the water. You can try a little experiment for yourself which might help you to understand. Spread out your fingers wide and pull your hand through a bowl of water. Your hand will slip through the water easily. Now close your fingers so that they are side by side, and pull your hand through the water again. This time you will find that it is harder to move your hand, but that you are making a much stronger, firmer movement. In just the same way, swimmers wearing flippers are able to swim very strongly.

TALES OF ANCIENT GREECE

Many thousand of years ago the Greeks believed in different gods and goddesses, who could control or explain away the natural events of life – the changing of the seasons, the coming of day or night, the reflecting powers of water . . . .

Adonis

Adonis was a very handsome young man indeed, the son of a woman who had been turned into a sweet-smelling tree. As he grew up, living in the countryside in total freedom, the goddess Aphrodite fell in love with him.

But one day Adonis was wounded by a boar and died. Aphrodite was so grief-stricken for her beautiful young man that Zeus, the supreme ruler of the heavens, decreed that for six months of the year Adonis could leave the underworld, the kingdom of the dead, and return to the earth.

So while Adonis spent six months in the underworld, the countryside was dead and barren too. But when he returned, the leaves unfurled and the flowers bloomed. In this way the Ancient Greeks resolved their questions about winter and summer.

Aphrodite

Aphrodite was very beautiful, and very powerful, too. She was the goddess of beauty and love, and the daughter of Zeus. At one time the Greeks thought of her as the goddess of gardens and calm seas. When Paris, a hero and soldier, desired the most beautiful woman in the world for his wife it was Aphrodite who found Helen for him, and thus began the Trojan War. Aphrodite also helped Jason gain the Golden Fleece.

Although she had many lovers, Aphrodite was said to be married to the god Hephaestus, and the mother of Eros.

Pandora

Pandora was the first woman on earth, according to the Ancient Greeks' beliefs. Zeus had become angry because Prometheus stole fire from the gods to give to men, and he ordered that an evil being be sent to earth to punish mankind. Pandora was created.

All the gods gave Pandora gifts (Pandora means all-gift); gifts of knowledge, beauty, cunning and flattery. She was also given curiosity, and a box which she was told never to open.

While she was on earth Pandora's curiosity grew until she could not contain it, and she opened the box. Out flew all the vices, sins, troubles and diseases of the world. She shut the lid quickly, but nothing remained except Hope. This was the Ancient Greeks' way of explaining the evils that pervaded the earth.

Narcissus

Narcissus was the son of the river god Cephisus, and he was very proud of his beauty. Many women loved him but in his vanity he paid them no attention. The young nymph, Echo, was so hurt by his coldness that she faded away until only her voice remained . . . which explained for the Greeks the cause of echoes.

But the young nymph's suffering had made the other gods angry, and they decided to punish Narcissus. They caused him to fall in love with his own reflection in a pool of clear water, and there he stayed, unable to leave, staring at his own face until eventually he died and turned into a flower, which was called Narcissus.

WEATHER REPORT

What are weather centres?

These are places, set up in many parts of the world, where information about weather is collected and classified on a regional and worldwide basis. The information – taken from weather balloons, ocean-going ships and planes, satellites, weather-ships and weather-stations based on land – has proved invaluable in the making of maps and weather-charts. Readings are taken every day. In main centres, such as airports, readings can be taken as often as once every thirty minutes.

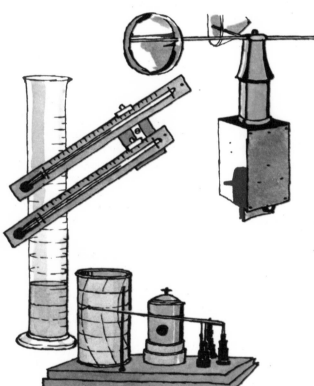

What equipment is used in weather-forecasting?

The *maximal and minimal thermometer* is used to take the highest and lowest temperatures of the day. It is shaded from direct sun by a screen called a *Stevenson's Screen*. The *rain-gauge* measures the amount of precipitation that has fallen, and the *barograph* continually measures the air pressure. It works by making a constant record with a pen on a chart. An *anometer* tests wind-speeds.

What is mist, fog and smog?

Mist occurs when warm, moist air cools and the moisture is condensed. Sometimes this falls as dew, but at others, such as still evenings, it remains in the air as mist, because the fine water particles are too small to be affected by gravity. Fog is similar to mist, but it is much denser, and more dangerous as visibility is much less. Smog is when fog becomes mixed with smoke of carbon-dioxide fumes from car engines, to form a thick, dirty-smelling atmosphere. Smog is now being controlled in many urban areas by the use of smokeless zones, but the problems of exhaust fumes still exist.

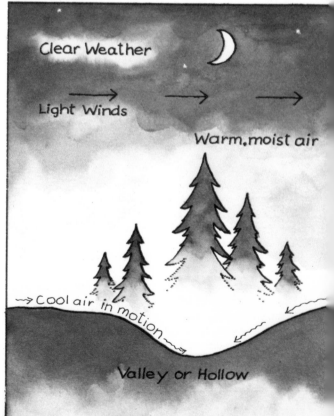

Clear Weather

Light Winds

Warm, moist air

Cool air in motion

Valley or Hollow

There are three types of rain.
Do you know what they are?

First there is *convectional rain*. This happens on a hot day when the sun heats the lower atmosphere and causes the air to rise. The water vapour in the air condenses when it reaches a certain height, and rain falls.

Relief rain is quite different. It occurs when moisture-bearing winds (those which have travelled across oceans) reach land and then must rise to cross mountains. In doing so, the moisture condenses, falling as rain on the peaks and their seaward side. The dry area inland is called the 'rainshadow' area.

Lastly there is *cyclonic rain*, caused when the warm front in a cyclone catches a cold front and rises above it (warm air being lighter than cold air). The moisture in the warm air condenses with cooling, and rain falls.

Clouds are often helpful
in weather-forecasting.
What are the main types?

There are Cirrus, Nimbus, Cumulus and Stratus clouds. Cirrus are sometimes known as 'mare's tails' – they are thin and wispy. Lying as high as 30,000 feet, they are ice-clouds and usually signal a depression, and rain. Nimbus are dark, full rain-clouds. Nimbus means 'rain-bearing'. Cumulus are the piled-up, cotton-wool clouds. Stratus are layered clouds, which do not necessarily forecast rain. Many clouds combine these different types: for instance, there are Cumulo-Nimbus, Cirrus-Stratus and Nimbus-Stratus cloud formations.

THE LEGENDS OF KING ARTHUR

Who was Arthur?

He was the hero of many tales and legends of the late Middle Ages, who became a mythical figure as the centuries passed and truth and fiction could not so easily be defined. What is believed, however, is that Arthur was a chief or leader of the Britons, who fought against the Saxon invasion during A.D. 400 and 500. That he had a castle, Camelot, is also believed; historians think it was probably in Somerset or Wales. But what is real history and what is merely myth is very hard to discover.

What was the legend of his life?

Arthur was supposed to have been the son of the King of the Britons, Uther Pendragon. Merlin, a magician, advised Uther Pendragon to hide his son from his enemies, and so he was brought up with a nobleman, Sir Ector.

Arthur became king after his father's death when he was able to pull the great sword Excalibur from a stone. Arthur established his court at Camelot and he married Guinevere, although Merlin warned him that one of his knights, Lancelot, loved Guinevere too.

While Arthur and Lancelot were fighting, Modred, a nephew of Arthur's, plotted a rebellion, as he wished to be king in Arthur's place. Although Arthur killed Modred, he was wounded himself. After the battle Arthur's fairy sister took him to the magical Vale of Avalon to heal him. According to legend, this is where he lies still, and should Britain be invaded again he will rise and fight once more.

What was the Round Table?

This was a large table used by Arthur and his 150 knights. It was round so that no knight would have a more honourable or important seat than another. The seats were called *sieges*. Among the knights of the Round Table were Lancelot, Gawain and Galahad. Galahad was known as the purest and noblest knight of all Arthur's knights. Gawain was Arthur's nephew. He and Lancelot became enemies when Lancelot killed his brothers by mistake. Gawain was killed fighting Modred.

What was the Holy Grail?

According to old legends this was a dish which had contained some of the blood of Christ. Brought to England by Joseph of Aramathea, it later disappeared, and the knights resolved to find it. Only those who had led pure lives could take part in this quest. When the Round Table was founded a special seat was set aside for the knight who could find the Grail. This seat was called the *Siege Perilous*.

Lancelot took part in the quest but, because of his guilty love for Guinevere, was unsuccessful. Only Galahad saw a full vision of the Grail, but it floated up to Heaven and was never seen again.

Who wrote the legends about Arthur?

The earliest-known reference to Arthur was made by a Welsh monk in A.D. 800, in his *History of the Britons*. During the 1100s Geoffrey of Monmouth published another history of the kings of Britain which mentioned Arthur, as well as a life-history of Merlin!

In the years that followed many poets and story-tellers created tales about Arthur, and these spread to many countries in Europe, and became more and more fantastic as time separated them from reality. One of the most famous romances about Arthur is Sir Thomas Malory's *Morte d'Arthur*, written in the thirteenth century.

Who was the Lady of the Lake?

A magical enchantress called Vivien, who lived in the lake and had powers over the sword Excalibur. In Malory's story, as Arthur is wounded at the end of his last battle, he throws the sword into the lake. An arm rises from the water to receive it, then both sword and arm disappear below the calm surface.

175

THE LOST CITIES: POMPEII AND HERCULANEUM

August 24, A.D. 79, was an ordinary summer's day for the people in the neighbouring Roman towns of Pompeii and Herculaneum. They went about their business, ate, talked, and walked the streets in the hot sunshine.

But less than a mile from the centre of Pompeii stood the dark shadow of the volcano Vesuvius. Although its slopes were rich with vineyards and it seemed to sleep, below the earth white-hot streams of lava rushed and bubbled, forcing themselves upwards . . . .

With a deafening roar the lava erupted from Vesuvius and swept down the mountainside into the towns of Herculaneum and Pompeii. There was no time for escape; two hundred people died trying to rush through one of Pompeii's exits, and many more died where they had fallen. After the lava came a soft white film of ash, covering the tragedy like snow.

In the silence of the summer's day nothing moved in either Pompeii or Herculaneum. Homes, streets, people, animals, all lay under the blanket of lava and ash. Soon rain came, and by some strange chance it acted with the ash to make a kind of cement, so that the victims and their lost cities were trapped forever.

Pompeii and Herculaneum lay like this for centuries, forgotten and abandoned until 1763, when the first real excavations were begun by an archaeologist called Giuseppe Fiorelli. Work has continued ever since then, the longest excavation in history. Yet even now there are parts of Pompeii and Herculaneum which are still to be discovered.

The fascinating thing about these cities is that they were not lost through the gradual passing of time. They were struck down in a single day, and because of the ash, left intact. Pompeii was a typical Roman city, well-laid-out with symmetrically planned streets. There was a theatre, pagan temples, industrial buildings, markets, baths, and everywhere were beautiful sculptures and paintings in the luxurious and comfortable homes. Pompeii provides an excellent view of the Roman Age, and it is a monument to the Romans which, because of a natural disaster, gives archaeologists valuable perception into the past. It is a real quirk of fate!

A QUESTION OF ART

What is chiaroscuro?

Chiaroscuro is the name of a technique whereby the artist makes great use of the contrast between light and shade to lend drama to his subject. One of the best known exponents of the technique was Rembrandt, who used it to great effect in his portraits and religious paintings. Other artists who have used it are Caravaggio, El Greco and Tintoretto. The word itself is taken from the Italian words meaning light and dark.

What is perspective?

Perspective is the art and science of making flat, two-dimensional drawings and paintings look three dimensional. The artist uses aerial and linear perspective to create an illusion of depth. With aerial perspective, objects are made lighter as they move further from the eye. With linear perspective, the object is made smaller as it approaches the horizon. The techniques of perspective were perfected during the Renaissance by artists like Leonardo da Vinci.

What is fresco?

Fresco is a method of painting on fresh plaster with water colours, and it is also the name of the finished product. Before starting a fresco, the artist makes a preliminary drawing, or cartoon, the exact size of the finished picture. Then he lays as much plaster as he can paint in a day on the surface. He traces the cartoon onto this and begins to paint as quickly as possible. He cannot paint on the plaster once it is dry. Fresco painting reached its peak during the Renaissance in Italy.

What is tempera?

Tempera is a painting medium consisting of powdered pigments, water, and either the yolk or the white of an egg. When properly applied in a series of layers it gives a semi-transparent finish and makes the colours extra brilliant. To prepare the surface to be painted, artists cover it with gesso, a special mixture of glue and chalk, and when finished the painting has great lasting qualities.

ANIMAL INFO

Are mute swans really silent?

The mute swan *is* a more or less silent bird, hence its name. It is a magnificent creature, widespread in Europe and North Asia, and is one of the heaviest birds able to fly, sometimes reaching weights of over 40lbs. Its graceful wing-span is between 7 and 8 feet, though one famous swan, known as 'Guardsman' attained a recorded wing span of 12 feet! Mute swans live in pairs for many years, building large nests and laying between 8 and 10 eggs, which hatch as grey cygnets. The birds usually get their stunning white plumage by the age of two.

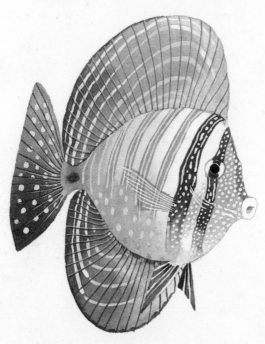

Why are surgeonfish so called?

Surgeonfish have a powerful weapon in the form of two blades or 'knives', embedded in the skin at the base of the caudal fin, used for attack as well as defence. These blades, which resemble surgeons' scalpels, give the fish their name.

What is an agama?

Agamas are an important group of lizards found mainly in Africa and Asia, with only one, the starred lizard, living in Europe. They are beautifully coloured when in the sunlight during the day, but turn a dull brown at night, when they enter their underground homes. They are very active creatures, and their speed and excellent vision means that they are very successful hunters, eating insects. They have a reputation for being quarrelsome, and will defend their own territories to the death.

How did the cowbird get its name?

The cowbird got its name because of its habit of following the huge herds of buffalo that once roamed the plains of North America, feeding on the many insects that were disturbed by the buffaloes' hoofs. It was also known as the buffalo bird. Now that the herds of buffalo are no more, the cowbirds fly in great flocks, descending on fields of ripening corn or rice and completely stripping acres of land, making them very unpopular with farmers. Cowbirds do not build a nest, but the female lays her single egg in the nest of another bird, hoping that the egg will be incubated (and the chick reared) by the unwitting foster-mother.

What is bee's wool?

This insect was so named because it was thought that it attacked and killed bees for food, but this has been proved to be untrue. It is sometimes found in abandoned hives, where it will feed on sick or dead bees, but it usually hunts and feeds on other, smaller insects. It grows to a length of about ½''.

Are flamingoes always pink?

The colouring of the flamingo's plumage depends on its diet. It eats tiny crustaceans, filtered from the water in its huge curved bill, and it is the colour of these minute creatures that determines the flamingo's colour—anything from palest pink to rosy red. In captivity, if the flamingo's usual food is not available, the plumage turns quite white.

MAKE MERRY MUSIC

What is a Sitar?

A sitar is a type of lute often played in India. The word comes from a Persian word meaning three-stringed, but in fact most sitars have four, five or even seven strings. The body of the instrument is shaped like a pear, and on the long neck are placed wire bars known as frets, which can be moved up and down to suit the way the music is played. The pegs which appear at the top of the neck of the instrument are used to tune the sitar, which is played on one string only for the melody, the others providing a background noise.

What is a Madrigal?

A Madrigal is a type of song, usually about some form of nature. They originated in Italy but became very popular in England during the 16th and 17th century. It is also known as a canzonet or ayre. At first they were sung unaccompanied and later they began to have a religious content. As time went on music was added, sometimes taking the place of one of the voices, and the madrigal was also included in several Gilbert and Sullivan operas.

Which well-known composer was deaf?

Ludwig Van Beethoven, who lived from 1770 to 1827. He was also a pianist, organist and violinist as well as a great composer. He wrote orchestral music, sonatas and chamber music, choral music and songs and one opera, *Fidelio*. Beethoven started to suffer from deafness in his late twenties, and the last thirty years of his life were spent in a world of silence; he was only able to hear musical notes in his own head. But he still retained his sense of humour and love of fun.

Can you name three percussion instruments?

The percussion group of instruments includes all instruments that you strike, so you can include the triangle, the xylophone, the glockenspiel and, of course, drums: from the tomtom and timpani to the African bell drum and the bass and side drums. Other popular percussion instruments are the tambourine, the cymbals and the gong.

IN THE WILD WEST

Here's a quiz to test your knowledge of the Wild West . . . .

1. What was Billy the Kid's real name, and the name of the man who eventually brought him to justice?

2. During the violent hey-day of the West, a man formed a detective agency which had considerable success in trapping outlaws and bank-robbers. What was his name?

3. Do you know who was nicknamed 'the deadly dentist'?

4. Who belonged to the infamous 'Hole in the Wall' gang?

5. What was the name of the sharp-shooting woman who appeared in Buffalo Bill's Wild West show?

6. Who was the judge in the small town of Fort Smith, Arkansas, who earned the name of 'hanging judge' after he condemned hundreds of men and women to the gallows during his term of office?

Check your answers on page 191

CROSSWORDS GALORE

The first crossword puzzle ever, appeared in the December 21st 1913 edition of the *New York World*. Arthur Wynne, a Liverpudlian who had emigrated to the States, hit upon the idea of developing the popular word square, in which words across and down read the same, into a puzzle in which there were across and down clues.

His first attempt, using a diamond shaped grid, was an instant success, and a crossword was soon a regular feature of this and other papers. The first to be published in Britain, also an Arthur Wynne puzzle, appeared in the *Sunday Express* in 1924, and was in the by then more common square format.

Prize puzzles—also known as pruzzles—became popular in the 1920s. In one example, the entrance fee each week was a shilling, and yet the takings amounted to over £1000 a day! There was just one prize of £1000.

Profits often lined the pockets of racketeers, but in some cases they went to worthy charities, as in the example of one contest in aid of the blind.

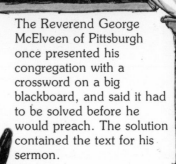

The Reverend George McElveen of Pittsburgh once presented his congregation with a crossword on a big blackboard, and said it had to be solved before he would preach. The solution contained the text for his sermon.

Perhaps the most famous crossword is *The Times* crossword, first printed on January 23, 1930. It was said that the Provost of Eton in the mid-30s used to time his boiled eggs by the time it took him to solve the daily puzzle. A less expert solver from Yorkshire wrote to the paper to say that he had tried boiling an egg in hope of inspiration, but that he had 'started at 8.00 and it is now 15.05 and the egg has burst'.

In 1926, a waiter in a coffee house in Budapest committed suicide. The police had to ask for help from the public in deciphering the suicide note, which was in the form of a crossword.

In 1944, M15 interrogated the chief crossword compiler for the *Daily Telegraph*, when five of the D-Day code names—UTAH, OMAHA, OVERLORD, MULBERRY and NEPTUNE—all appeared as solutions within the space of a month.

They again made investigations when ARTILLERY ROW, the name of the road outside Wormwood Scrubs, turned up in *The Times* crossword just two days before the famous spy George Blake escaped from the same prison by going over the wall.

There have been many different shapes and forms of crossword, of varying difficulty. One Englishman from Surrey even compiled a huge, three-dimensional crossword with 3375 'squares', or should it be cubes? The puzzle, constructed in a 15 × 15 × 15 framework, took two years to compile, and had three types of clues: across, down and through!

Margaret Petherbridge Farrar, co-editor of the first book of crossword puzzles in 1924, was to receive a strange letter of complaint some time later when she was crossword editor for the *New York Times*.

The solution to one clue 'To succeed' should have been 'To make a go of', but in the paper there was no indication as to the breaks between words, and the answer had been read as 'To make a goof' by the poor complainant!

Crosswords were forbidden in Paris at one point during the Second World War, in case they should be used by fifth columnists.

GUESS WHO?

The short life-stories below all belong to famous writers. Do you know who they are?

1. He was born in Dublin in 1882, and graduated from University College before studying medicine in Paris. Although very much an Irishman, he only returned to Ireland twice after leaving; once for his mother's burial, once for his wedding. His most famous book, *Ulysses*, took him seven years to write and was banned in America. He suffered increasingly from blindness before his death in 1941.

2. She lived a very quiet life, her first twenty five years being spent at her father's rectory in Hampshire. It was there that she wrote her first novel, *Pride and Prejudice*. Later her family moved to Bath, where some of her work is set, and after her father's death she stayed with her mother and sister until her death in 1817. She never married, and although she gained little acclaim from her books while she was alive, they're regarded as classics today.

3. He was an American, born in San Francisco in 1876. When he was 17 he took to the sea and saw Japan and the Bering Sea while serving as an able seaman. After this he tried his hand at many different things: he was an oyster pirate, a gold-prospector in the Klondike Gold Rush, and a war correspondent in the Russo-Japanese war. He began to write books about his adventures, *The Call of the Wild* being perhaps his best-known. He was a socialist, and felt deeply the injustices of his time. He died at the early age of forty in 1916.

4. She wrote under a male pseudonym, and her early life was not an easy one. Born into an aristocratic family in France, she was brought up by a stern grandmother and then entered into an unhappy marriage which ended when she fled to Paris with her two children to obtain a divorce. It was then, to support herself and her children, that she took up writing, and in the course of her lifetime she wrote up to eighty novels in all, the best-known being *The Haunted Pool*. She was very concerned with the issue of women's rights, and was a tireless crusader for equality. During her life Amandine Aurore Lucie Dupin, Baronne Dudevant (to give her her proper name) was very close to the great musician Chopin.

Check your answers on page 191

TRUE OR FALSE?

1. Julius Caesar gave news of his victory with the words "Veni, vidi, vici" – I came, I saw, I conquered. True or false?

2. Edmund Hillary and Tenzing Norkay were the first men to conquer Everest. True or false?

3. William Shakespeare was born in Stratford-upon-Avon. True or false?

4. 'The Book of Kells' is an illuminated copy of the Gospels in Latin. True or false?

5. Rembrandt actually painted some sixty self-portraits. True or false?

6. "Nature Morte" is an artists' expression meaning Impressionism. True or false?

7. Davy Crockett died fighting at the Battle of the Little Big Horn. True or false?

8. The D.S.O. award for bravery stands for "Distinguished Service Order". True or false?

9. The city of Leningrad was formerly called St. Petersburg. True or false?

10. St. Bernard is traditionally associated with Christmas in Europe. True or false?

11. The Bridge of Sighs is in Rome. True or false?

12. Billy The Kid's real name was William Bonney. True or false?

13. The river Orinoco is in Botswana. True or false?

14. 'Lippizzaner' is the name given to a special kind of horse. True or false?

15. Rubber begins its life as a gummy juice called latex. True or false?

16. This is the the correct way to spell 'inflamatory'. True or false?

17. The Russian Crown Jewels are kept in the Palace of Arms, within the Kremlin. True or false?

18. Mark Twain's real name was Samuel Langhorne Clemens. True or false?

19. Big Ben first came into use in 1859. True or false?

20. A 'Stradivarius' is a famous kind of cello. True or false?

Check your answers on page 191

DISASTER!

Which disaster began in Pudding Lane?

In the early hours of the morning, during September 1666, fire broke out in a bakery in Pudding Lane, east of London Bridge, after a long drought. Fanned by an easterly gale, the flames soon spread across the city: 13,000 houses, 84 churches, and countless other buildings were destroyed in the blaze, which lasted four days, and was seen as far away as Oxford.

Incredibly, only eight died, and in two crucial ways the Great Fire actually proved beneficial, cleansing the worst plague areas, and allowing at least part of London to be rebuilt by Christopher Wren.

When was the San Francisco Earthquake?

San Francisco lies along the notorious San Andreas Fault in California, a geological split in the Earth's surface. At 5.15am on **18th April 1906,** the first of several massive tremors split streets and collapsed buildings throughout the city.

A giant tidal wave hit the waterfront, and fractured electricity cables and gas mains, starting fires which burned for three days. 25,000 buildings were lost, and almost £150,000,000 of damage caused, although miraculously less than 500 people died.

What was the last great airship disaster?

Airships, dirigible aircraft using lighter than air gas to stay airborne and propellers for directional flight, flew more than 50 years before the first aeroplane. Germany pioneered airship passenger travel, under Count Zeppelin, between 1910-14, carrying nearly 35,000 passengers without fatality.

Destruction of the British R101 (1930), and the American *Akron* (1933), among others, however, resulted in complete abandonment of commercial airships, except in Germany. The *Hindenburg,* the largest airship ever built (1926), was totally destroyed in May 1937, when an explosion on board ignited its hydrogen envelope. The last great airship, the *Graf Zeppelin,* withdrew from service in 1938.

Why did the Titanic sink?

The *Titanic* was the largest and most luxurious liner of her time when she set out on her maiden, transatlantic voyage in April 1912 with 2,200 passengers and crew. Despite reports of icebergs in the vicinity, the *Titanic* maintained her speed of 22 knots and struck an iceberg which tore a 300-foot gash in her hull.

Described by her makers as unsinkable, the ship was capable of remaining afloat with two of her sixteen watertight compartments flooded, but six were in fact holed. Insufficient warning to abandon ship and inadequate lifeboat space meant that only 705 people survived.

ALL CREATURES GREAT AND SMALL

Which is the world's largest land animal?

The largest land animal without any doubt is the elephant. The Indian elephant has a concave forehead and the African elephant has a convex forehead, but both male and female elephants have ivory tusks. Because of their great strength elephants are often used to push or pull heavy weights such as timber logs and this is especially true of the Indian elephant. An elephant can eat as much as half a ton of food a day and likes to be near water, both for drinking and washing purposes.

What is so special about a Przewalski's horse?

It is the only true remaining wild horse left living in a natural habitat. It was discovered in the late 19th century by the man whose name it bears, roaming wild and free in central Asia. It can still be found in Mongolia today in small numbers, but to make sure that the breed does not become entirely extinct it can also be seen in many zoos, and if bred successfully several may be returned to the steppes to live in a real wild state.

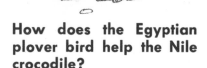

How does the Egyptian plover bird help the Nile crocodile?

By picking the morsels of food from between the crocodile's teeth and so helping to keep the teeth clean. In thus helping the crocodile, the plover bird also gets food for itself. Crocodiles will snap at the hand of a man but they allow the plover to pick out leeches and other larvae from their teeth without harming them at all. This strange friendship between these two creatures has existed for many years.

Which is the tallest animal in the world?

The giraffe; the male giraffe can be as much as eighteen feet tall. They use their long necks and tongues to bite off the leaves from tall trees, but they have very poor voices and can only manage a low *'bleat bleat'* occasionally. They are fleet of foot when danger threatens, but if provoked to fight they attack their enemies with their sharp hooves, which can prove very dangerous.

The young of which animal is called a 'joey'?

The kangaroo, one of those large bounding mammals which live in Australia and New Guinea. The Great Grey Kangaroo lives in the forests and feeds on grass and leaves, while the Red Kangaroo prefers the highlands. Smaller kangaroos are known as wallabies and there is even a tree kangaroo with specially adapted padded feet for safe tree-climbing. All female kangaroos carry their young in pouches until they are able to look after themselves and a group of kangaroos living together is known as a 'mob'.

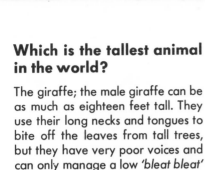

What is a Lodgepole?

An Eastern Chipmunk found in the woodlands of the eastern United States and Canada. These cheeky little creatures like trees, unlike other members of the chipmunk family who prefer the ground. They eat fruit and berries, often storing food in their cheeks until it is safe to eat it if they are pursued by predators. They live in underground burrows made up of a network of tunnels and passages.

IT'S TRUE!

The average man can expect to live for 68 years, fourteen of which will be spent at work and twenty-one asleep. His heart will beat 2,500,000,000 times, he will take 600,000,000 breaths, speak 20,000,000 words, walk 128,000 miles, grow 35 feet of hair and 27 feet of beard. To sustain himself he will eat the equivalent of 20 pigs, 300 chickens, 6,000 loaves, 8,000 lbs of sugar, 9,000 lbs of potatoes and 10,000 eggs, all washed down with 18,000 pints of milk and 850 lbs of tea and coffee.

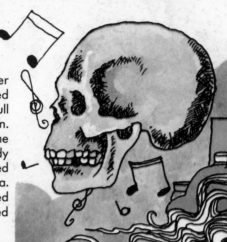

The famous Austrian composer Haydn, who died in 1809, was buried in a tomb at Eisenstadt, but the skull inside the tomb is not his own. Haydn's skull was stolen from the tomb a few days after the body was interred and is now preserved in the Musical Society of Vienna. The authorities mistakenly seized another man's skull and replaced it in Haydn's tomb.

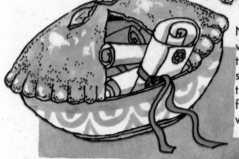

Nursery rhymes often seem nonsensical, but they are not. Jack Horner was steward to the Abbot of Glastonbury at the time King Henry ordered the dissolution of the monasteries. In an attempt to escape trial the abbot sent 12 property deeds to the king hidden in a large pie. Jack Horner took the deed for Mells Manor out before delivering the pie and his family still live there today. The king rejected the bribe and the abbot was hanged.

The natives of the Basasari tribe of Togo, West Africa, have a unique way of naming their children. They place the favourite foods of their ancestors on a table and let the child choose which one he wants. He assumes the name of the ancestor whose favourite food it was.

Scientists stopped using the period taken by the earth to circle the sun as a standard unit of time in 1956 when it was discovered that the earth is slowing down and we have already lost two seconds this century. They now use atom clocks that are accurate to one second every 1,000 years.